The Leverage of National Board Candidacy

An Exploration of Teacher Learning

The Leverage of National Board Candidacy

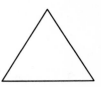

An Exploration of Teacher Learning

Jana Lynn Hunzicker

Foreword by Mary Ann Manos

Universal Publishers
Boca Raton, Florida

The Leverage of National Board Candidacy:
An Exploration of Teacher Learning

Universal Publishers
Boca Raton, Florida • USA
2006

ISBN: 1-58112- 941-6

www.universal-publishers.com

To Anne, Barbara, and Jamie

Contents

Foreword

Without a doubt, it was the most difficult task I have ever accomplished! The year I spent earning National Board Certification in Early Adolescent/English Language Arts demanded more professionalism, greater endurance, and heightened classroom creativity than 25 years in the public school classroom, a master's degree, the Texas Career Ladder, or my doctoral dissertation. I was stretched to the limit, and I reveled in it. I found that the NBPTS certification process offered several levels of challenge as well as support and influence.

Having been a faculty member of higher education for five years, I came back to the elementary school classroom to validate my teaching mastery and to renew my teacher's heart. As refreshing as the experience proved to be, I found myself running to keep up with daily instruction, discipline, administrative tasks, parent communication, and professional interactions. I also found the precise NBPTS writing criteria to be extensive and demanding. My first video tapes were a disaster! On the other hand, the encouragement of classroom colleagues surrounded me.

Well-wishers abound for NBPTS candidates, and they are swept along knowing that they are doing something very important. Interactions with other educators seem to take on a positive tone, far from the usual griping of the faculty lounge. I found the support from building and district administrators strengthening. Even the greater state and national educational community was aware that I was attempting a new level of professionalism. Support came from everywhere, even if some scratched their heads in bewilderment over a college professor who sought to earn the highest certification a classroom teacher can achieve.

Finally, I was certified. I stood shoulder-to-shoulder with the best in the nation, and I couldn't stop smiling. It took two years to accomplish my goal, but the effort was well worth the time I invested.

National Board certification opens many doors of influence. NBCTs who wish to stay in the classroom do so with a new sense of validation and expertise, their work proven by the most rigorous test any educator can seek. I congratulate them. Our children are greatly blessed through their service. NBCTs who want to stretch their influence into school and district leadership have that opportunity as they are sought out to mentor new National Board candidates. NBCTs who wish to investigate the forum of higher education find open doors to teach courses for others who seek graduate credit during their NBPTS certification year. Most state boards of education seek NBCTs as contributors to teacher certification or ethics boards, and national platforms are available for NBCTs as consultants with content area associations, higher education accreditation, or national standards design. Today, NBCTs design in-service sessions, conduct presentations at national conferences, and publish books – all on the basis of their National Board work. They serve at all echelons of American schooling and administration. Perhaps soon, a NBCT will serve as a school superintendent – taking teaching excellence into CEO leadership.

In *The Leverage of National Board Candidacy*, Dr. Hunzicker provides a detailed portrait of three teachers seeking National Board certification. Her scholarly work is unequaled in the precise description of outstanding teaching and accompanying thought processes of this incredibly difficult endeavor. This book must be read by all who are considering or attempting National Board certification, as well as by those who have earned the certification. The heart and wisdom of stellar teachers is written into every section of this text.

Dr. Mary Ann Manos, NBCT
Associate Professor, Bradley University, Peoria, IL

Author's Note

Social constructivism is the idea that individuals "make sense" of the world by attributing meaning to their experiences. Each new experience or interaction influences what we know and believe to be true. Because our exposure to new information is constant, we are in a continual state of learning, growth, and change. Of course, all information to which we are exposed is filtered through our prior knowledge, experiences, and beliefs, causing individual quests for learning to proceed along varied paths and assorted timelines.

When new information or experiences align closely with what we already know or believe, our ideas of truth are reinforced. However, when new information and experiences conflict with our previous notions, we are not comfortable until we resolve the differences. We do this one of three ways: We deny the new information, we find data that supports what we believe so that we can disregard what does not align, or we modify our knowledge and/or beliefs to fit with the new information to which we have been exposed. This is how we learn.

The Leverage of National Board Candidacy is written so that the reader, individually or in collaboration with others, can construct her own ideas about teacher learning through the process of National Board certification. The opportunity for the social construction of knowledge is at the heart of this book.

Part One:
Establishing the Context

1

Approaching
National Board Candidacy

The National Board for Professional Teaching Standards (NBPTS), founded in 1987, is a nonprofit, nonpartisan, independently governed body of 63 directors, the majority of whom are practicing classroom teachers. Created for the purpose of "delineating outstanding practice and recognizing those who achieve it" (NBPTS, 2004, p. v), teachers may currently seek National Board certification in 24 different specialty areas. To be eligible to pursue the certification, a teacher must hold a bachelor's degree and a valid teaching license, and have completed at least three years of teaching at the early childhood, elementary, middle, or high school level (NBPTS, 2004).

Guided by five core propositions, the NBPTS certification process involves two requirements: a performance-based portfolio and a written assessment. The portfolio consists of four entries that document classroom teaching through videotapes, samples of student work, and written analyses of teaching practice. The written assessment, a three hour, timed essay test where candidates demonstrate knowledge within their certification specialty, takes place at a NBPTS-approved testing center (NBPTS, 2003). The entire certification process takes a minimum of 200 hours to complete (NBPTS, 2003), although some candidates have spent 300 to 400 hours on the process (Hunzicker, 2003a; NBPTS, 2002).

The standards of the NBPTS are "designed to capture the craft, artistry, proficiency, and understandings - both deep and broad - that contribute to the complex work that is accomplished teaching" (NBPTS, 2004, p. 3). In addition, research confirms that teachers who have experienced the process consider it to be an outstanding means of professional development. One team of researchers writes, "Teachers routinely rate the process as more powerful than that of advanced university coursework or short-term trainings, citing the sustained analysis and reflection of their teaching practice required to meet portfolio entry requirements" (Linquanti & Peterson, 2001, p. 4). Candidates who are not successful in accomplishing the certification during their first attempt can "bank" their scores and continue working toward the goal for up to two years. For this reason, National Board certification is considered a three year process.

The number of teachers seeking National Board certification has grown dramatically each year since its inception in 1993. As of November 2003, 65,000 teachers across the United States had voluntarily completed the certification requirements (Goldhaber & Anthony, 2004). During the 2003-2004 school year, 19,742 teachers nationwide pursued the certification (Sandy-Hanson, personal communication, February 10, 2006), and by November 2005, the United States boasted a total of 47,913 National Board certified teachers (NBCTs) (NBPTS, 2006). By 2010, the NBPTS expects to certify 100,000 additional teachers, resulting in total certification of approximately 3% of the United States teaching force (Darling-Hammond, 2001).

Becoming a NBCT is not easily accomplished. Only about one third of candidates earn the certification on their first attempt. During the 2004-2005 school year, only 36% of first-time candidates nationwide were successful in earning the certification (Sandy-Hanson, personal communication, February 10, 2006), and the achievement rate is just slightly higher for candidates reapplying for the process. The relatively low achievement rate is a stark indicator of the rigor required in order to earn National Board certification.[1] Regardless of whether or not certification is achieved, teachers who have completed the process report that it results in strengthened teaching practice. In particular, teachers identify improved skills in:

1.) reflection and analysis (Bohen, 2001; Center for the Future of Teaching and Learning [CFTL], 2002; Chittenden & Jones, 1997; Lustick, 2002; Moseley & Rains, 2003; NBPTS, 2002; Sato, 2000; Tracz, Sienty, Todorov, Snyder, Takashima, Pensabene, Olsen, Pauls, & Sork, 1995; Tracz, Daughtry, Henderson-Sparks, Newman, & Sienty, 2005; Vandevoort, Amrein-Beardsley, & Berliner, 2004),

2.) increased collaboration with colleagues (Anderson, Hancock, & Jaus, 2001; Athanases, 1994; Chittenden & Jones, 1997; Kieffer-Barone, Mulvaney, Hillman, & Parker, 1999; Mitchell, 1998; NBPTS, 2001b; Sato, 2000),

3.) expanded methods of student assessment (Athanases, 1994; CFTL, 2001; Mitchell, 1998; NBPTS, 2001b; Tracz et al., 2005), and

4.) greater clarity of underlying assumptions and beliefs (Athanases, 1994; Chittenden & Jones, 1997; Sato, 2000) as key areas of learning.

Moreover, the first scientific study of teacher learning during National Board candidacy supports teachers' widespread claims that the NBPTS certification process is a worthwhile form of professional development. Lustick and Sykes (2006) found that teachers do indeed learn as a result of the NBPTS experience. In their study, 120 science teachers learned the most in regard to emphasizing the principles and practices of the scientific method in their daily teaching practice and utilizing ongoing student assessment to guide instructional decisions.

---

[1]Some or all of the data in the research described herein was provided by the National Board for Professional Teaching Standards. All conclusions stated in this book are those of the author, and no endorsement by the National Board for Professional Teaching Standards should be implied.

The Leverage of National Board Candidacy

While achievement of National Board certification requires a great deal of professional skill, intelligence, effort, and perseverance, teachers who make the choice to pursue the certification tend to be highly motivated to learn and grow professionally. Three such teachers, Anne, Barbara, and Jamie, sought NBPTS certification as Middle Childhood Generalists during the 2004-2005 school year.

Ranging in age from 42 to 55, all three Illinois teachers taught in financially healthy, large suburban school districts during their certification year. In order to explore their learning throughout the experience, the three teachers were interviewed seven times and observed teaching in their classrooms four times between November 2004 and November 2005. In addition, each teacher's principal and two students were interviewed, and samples of student work were collected. Through Anne's, Barbara's, and Jamie's experiences during National Board candidacy, we gain a great deal of insight regarding the learning that occurs for teachers during the pursuit of National Board certification. Their stories begin here.

Anne

Anne, currently in her sixteenth year as a teacher, did not begin her teaching career until she was 39 years old. Waiting until her children were in junior high and high school, she returned to college at age 36, earning a bachelor's degree in Psychology with state certification in Elementary Education.

Anne has always taught fifth grade. During her first two years in the teaching profession, she taught in a small, rural school located near her home in the country; but with two years of experience, she accepted employment in the nearby city of Knollcrest to earn a higher salary. Teaching in Knollcrest School District 802 for the next four years, Anne knew that she eventually wanted to teach at the district's gifted magnet school because of its outstanding reputation. When she transferred to Dickenson Gifted School at the beginning of her fifth year in District 802, she enrolled in a graduate program and earned a master's degree in Gifted Education.

Anne's principal, who has worked closely with her for the past five years, describes Anne as well respected by others. "Students, parents, and colleagues listen to her, and parents request her because they believe their children will have a positive learning experience in her classroom," she comments.

The 2004-2005 school year marks Anne's tenth year at Dickenson. She describes Dickenson as a school that exposes students to music and the arts while at the same time providing academics accelerated by one grade level. Anne considers the Dickenson faculty to be a group of hardworking, knowledgeable professionals. "There is not one lazy teacher on the staff," she remarks. "As far as committee work and school improvement, we're all involved. The teachers here go above and beyond with everything they do. You constantly hear people talking and planning together, and since it's a small school everyone knows every child."

Anne describes her current class, made up of 24 fifth graders, as the most difficult group of students she has ever been assigned because they are less mature and of lower academic ability than students she has had in the past. "This is the class everyone's talked about," she notes. "As I've watched them come up through the grades, I've always thought, 'Oh, their teachers look so stressed', and now I'm their teacher!" One unique characteristic of the group is a significant gender imbalance. Anne's class consists of 17 boys and 7 girls.

Anne first heard about National Board certification when it was advertised by her school district. Teachers at Dickenson began talking about it, and Anne recalls getting caught up in the excitement of a new challenge when a colleague encouraged her to participate. "It seems like every four years I get itchy and want to make a change," she observes, pointing out that she has transferred schools, earned a master's degree, and become a teacher of gifted students in order to maintain a high level of professional stimulation throughout her career. "I wasn't willing to make a change that might take me away from Dickenson, so I thought National Board certification was a good opportunity," she reflects.

A group of eight teachers, including Anne, made the commitment to pursue the certification during the 2003-2004 school year. "I went into it blindly," she recalls, remembering that the process was much more involved than she had anticipated. Although she was ready to proceed, extenuating circumstances prevented her from completing the certification requirements during her first attempt. Due to the illness and passing of her father, Anne made the decision to formally withdraw, postponing her efforts until the following school year. When she began the certification process the second time, she felt much better prepared since she was already familiar with the requirements. "In addition," she explains, "when I saw my class, I realized that even if state funding didn't pay my registration fee I was going to do it because I needed help becoming a better teacher for this unique bunch of kids."

"I know she'll complete this successfully," comments Anne's principal in January. "Anne is a person who sets a goal and then goes forth and achieves it. When I think of National Board certified teachers, Anne is one of them. I can't imagine her not becoming certified. If there were a commercial advertising National Board certified teachers, she'd be the person!"

Barbara

Barbara, in her nineteenth year of teaching in Knollcrest District 802, has taught all grade levels from kindergarten through fifth grade. While she has spent most of her career teaching third and fourth grade students, she also served the district as a reading specialist for seven years. Holding a bachelor's degree in Elementary Education and a master's degree in Reading, she has completed 48 semester hours of graduate work beyond her master's. Barbara is also trained in Reading Recovery.

While she has worked in six different schools in District 802, Barbara left the reading department to join the staff at Cady Stanton Elementary School when it opened in 2000. "I wanted to get back into the classroom, and I also wanted to be part of a school that was making a difference," she explains. Barbara identifies a professional development experience that began during her first year at Cady Stanton as particularly influencing her teaching practice. "We're a Ball Foundation school, and we decided to select a few teachers interested in making an impact on student achievement. I was one of four who volunteered to do that," she explains. "Our goal was to teach using best practices supported by research, and we decided to focus on reading and writing workshop. We started by reading professional books, and then began trying things in our classrooms."

"I've made a lot of changes in my teaching as a result of that experience," Barbara reflects. "Especially because of the readings and the support of my colleagues in the group, I was able to make changes in my classroom that I'd wanted to make for a long time. After we implemented the workshop model in our own classrooms, our whole school followed suit because people liked what we were doing and wanted to know more about it. The voluntary style of professional development worked very, very well for Cady Stanton. I was on the ground floor of doing it, and I loved it!"

Barbara's principal of three years, who knew her socially and worked with her on district-wide committees for several years before coming to Cady Stanton, describes Barbara as having an outstanding reputation as a classroom teacher. "Parents request her because she maintains close communication with families, and her fellow fourth grade teachers look to her for advice," she remarks. "Her students achieve very well in comparison to the other fourth grade classes," she adds. "In the area of literacy, Barbara's students shine."

The 2004-2005 school year marks Barbara's fifth year as a teacher at Cady Stanton. Currently teaching fourth grade, she has a class of 28 students. "We have probably the strongest staff in the district," Barbara describes of her colleagues. "The teachers here are interested in increasing student achievement and participate in lots of professional development; and our principal is very dynamic, very bright. She remembers what it's like to be in the classroom, so she is always supportive."

The Leverage of National Board Candidacy

Barbara recalls that about seven years ago, information about National Board certification was sent to all District 802 teachers via e-mail. "I thought it sounded like something I wanted to do," she remembers, "but I didn't want to take the written assessment. I don't like standardized tests at all, so that's what held me back. Plus, obtaining the grant money sounded like a real hassle." But six years later, Barbara reconsidered. Approaching retirement, she was interested in increasing her salary during the last three years of her teaching career. "The state stipend is $3, 000 a year, and District 802 pays a percentage of the base salary," she explains, "so I found out more about it. I realized that I had the background experience to be able to accomplish it, and that gave me confidence. I decided to give it a try." After completing the registration process, Barbara was pleased to learn that another teacher at Cady Stanton had decided to seek the certification as well.

Barbara shares that she is motivated toward National Board certification because she believes it will increase her credibility as a teacher. "It will give me free reign in my classroom," she comments. "I will feel more comfortable trying things that I might not otherwise try. I might decide not to do a particular lesson just because it's in the textbook, and do something I feel is more effective instead. If I am NBPTS certified I can say, 'I am certified in this area, and I feel that this is a better choice.' It gives me that authority."

When Barbara's principal learned that she was pursuing National Board certification, she was very pleased. "I think Barbara will be successful because she perseveres," she predicts. "Barbara is a person who will work really hard at it. She's very organized, very detailed, and very well written. I don't think she'll have any trouble explaining what she does in her classroom every day."

Jamie

Jamie is in her twentieth year as a fifth grade teacher. "It's probably unusual to stay at one grade level all this time," she comments, "but I like fifth grade!" In her twenty years as a teacher, Jamie has always taught in Saxon School District 66. After spending 14 years teaching in one

22

building, she became a member of the original Cassatt Grade School (CGS) faculty when the new school opened six years ago. "I wanted Jamie to be a part of opening our new building," her principal states. "She's a great teacher, and I think she's good for kids." Jamie holds a bachelor's degree in Elementary Education and a master's degree in Curriculum and Instruction.

Her principal, who has known her for 18 years and been her principal for 11, describes Jamie as 100% professional. "She spends more time than anyone else at CGS on what she's doing in her classroom," he notes. "Jamie would be happy if every morning the kids came in and the rest of the world went away until 3:15 p.m. She just wants to teach kids." One reason that Jamie is devoted to teaching is because she enjoys it so much. She remarks, "When teaching is no longer fun, I'll find something else to do!"

"Jamie is a teacher who proves herself to parents over time," her principal describes. While parents rarely request her, they are usually pleased with their child's learning experience by the end of the school year. "The kids in Jamie's classroom do a lot of work, but her expectations are always well articulated to the kids and to the parents," he notes. "The work they do is very project-oriented, and Jamie's timelines for work completion are very reasonable. By the end of the school year, parents realize that their children learned a lot and that they're ready for junior high."

Jamie, in her sixth year at CGS, describes it as a friendly school. "It's very academically oriented," she comments. "We have a lot of camaraderie between the teachers, and that sets a positive tone for the whole school." While Jamie considers the CGS staff to be enthusiastic and easy to work with, she admits that she prefers to work independently. "Efforts to collaborate with others and work on committees are really not me," she explains. "I just like to teach and be left alone."

Jamie's fifth grade class consists of 23 students, 8 girls and 15 boys. Although in previous years she has been responsible for teaching gifted and learning disabled students within her regular division classroom, her current class is made up of students who fall within the normal range of academic ability. However, Jamie notes the immaturity of the class, commenting that she has to make extra efforts to keep them focused. "It has something to do with the fact that there are more boys than girls," she hypothesizes. "Also, there are no leaders in this group."

When two of Jamie's friends finished their master's degrees in May 2003, one of their professors encouraged them to consider National Board certification. "She told them that it would give them a chance to move up on the pay scale, and it would be wise to complete the requirements while they were still in school mode," Jamie recalls. "I wanted to take more graduate courses, but there weren't any left to take; and then, watching them go through National Board certification, I thought, 'Well, it's a good experience, and it's about the only thing I haven't tried yet.' I also liked the monetary incentive offered by the state, so I started looking for information about it."

Jamie learned more about the certification on the NBPTS website and then contacted her friends' professor at a local university to help her get started. She was pleased when the professor told her that another friend of hers had also decided to pursue the certification. "We're kind of doing this together," Jamie explains early in the 2004-2005 school year.

While the financial incentives offered by the state and her school district were appealing motivators in Jamie's decision to pursue the certification, she also hopes it will make her a better teacher. Moreover, Jamie likes the idea that the master teaching certificate held by NBCTs is valid in all 50 states, since she and her husband have considered relocating.

When Jamie's principal learned that she had decided to seek National Board certification, he was surprised that she was interested in pursuing something so high profile since she is a person who tends to keep to herself. But after he thought about it, the idea made sense to him. "When Jamie decides to do something, she goes after it until she's conquered it," he remarks.

A Purpose for Reading

The Leverage of National Board Candidacy is organized into two sections. Capturing the teaching and certification experiences of Anne, Barbara, and Jamie during the 2004-2005 school year, Part One establishes a personalized context for exploring teacher learning through National Board candidacy. Chapters 2, 3, and 4 exemplify the teaching practices, guiding philosophies, and thought processes of the three teachers during their certification year while Chapter 5 illustrates the conditions, highlights, and challenges of each teacher's certification experience.

With a personalized context established, Part Two explores teacher learning through National Board candidacy as it occurred for Anne, Barbara, and Jamie. After detailing each teacher's personal account of learning during the certification process, Chapter 6 synthesizes the three teachers' learning experiences before comparing them to the findings of recently conducted research. Focusing on Jamie's difficult learning experience, Chapter 7 explores the varying nature and degree of the three teachers' learning in comparison to other studies. In closing, Chapter 8 assimilates the ideas presented in Chapters 6 and 7 by defining and describing the leverage of National Board candidacy on teacher learning.

By establishing a personalized context, considering each teacher's account of learning, and comparing these accounts to recently conducted studies on the topic, the reader will be prepared to construct her own ideas about National Board candidacy and the learning that takes place for teachers through the experience.

2

Anne: Creative, Caring, Respectful

Knollcrest School District 802, located in a community of 112, 000, operates 37 public schools that serve 14, 245 students in grades kindergarten through twelve. The district employs 974 full time teachers and other certified staff, 46% of whom hold a master's degree or higher. Eleven teachers employed by District 802 are National Board certified.

Dickenson Gifted School, a first through fifth grade gifted magnet school in the district, houses a population of 265 students from across the city of Knollcrest. With a certified staff of 15 teachers, 67% of the Dickenson faculty have a master's degree or higher, and two teachers in the school are National Board certified. While 63.4% of the students enrolled at Dickenson are white, 21.5% are black, and 15% are Hispanic, Asian/Pacific Islander, or Native American. In addition, 29% of Dickenson students are eligible for free or reduced lunch according to federal guidelines, and no students at the school receive services for Limited English Proficiency (LEP) or special education. The school's attendance rate averages 95.4%, with an annual mobility rate of 4.6%. Student achievement is very strong at Dickenson. In 2003 and 2004, 95% of students in grades three, four, and five met or exceeded standards on the Illinois Standards Achievement Test (ISAT).

Anne's fifth grade classroom, called the Van Gogh Café, is located on the second floor of the school. Down a long main corridor and up a heavy flight of stairs, the room is easily noticed due to the prominent hand-drawn sign announcing the name of the classroom as well as the renditions of Van Gogh paintings displayed on and around the door leading inside. Within Anne's classroom, the Van Gogh theme continues. Two hand-painted awnings hang inward above the large windows of the room, creating a curbside view. One is a replica of Van Gogh's *Starry, Starry Night* while the second is painted to resemble *Monday Wash* by Jonathan Green. In addition, several Van Gogh prints, as well as renditions of artwork from other famous artists, are displayed around the classroom in both two-dimensional and three-dimensional form.

Beyond the replicas of fine art, a variety of written and numerical information enlivens Anne's classroom. High on one wall is a banner that reads, "The question is to think..." Underneath it, six posters displaying Bloom's Taxonomy are prominent. Several larger posters are on display as well, outlining the steps of multiplication and division and reminding students of key words to use when explaining mathematical procedures in writing. A small word wall containing about 50 difficult words is located near the pencil sharpener, and a number line of positive and negative integers outlining the numerical progression from trillions to trillionths claims at least ten feet of wall space. Between the windows, a large city map of Knollcrest, divided into wards, is available for exploration.

Anne's desk and accompanying tables, bookshelves, and file cabinets are centered on the long wall opposite the windows, facing the class. A TV/VCR/DVD player is mounted high on the wall at the front center of the classroom. On the shorter wall to the right of her desk is an overhead projector and screen, and a chalkboard covers the wall at the far end of the room. On either side of the chalkboard are two doors, one leading into a cloak room and the other leading to a small storage area. A compact classroom library of trade books, organized by category, is housed in a double bookcase off to one side.

The following vignettes capture glimpses of Anne's teaching practices, guiding philosophies, and thought processes during her NBPTS certification year. Organized into four categories, the narratives collectively provide a candid representation of a creative, caring, and respectful teacher during her year of National Board candidacy.

Communication and Instructional Delivery

"We're going to be doing a juggling act this afternoon," Anne announces right after lunch on a bright day in January. Explaining that she and her student teacher are going to be teaching small groups while others in the class work at their desks, she says, "I thought I'd go over your vocabulary homework so you can work on it independently if you have time."

The assignment integrates the week's vocabulary words with *The Giver* by Lois Lowery, a novel the class has just finished reading. On the chalkboard, Anne writes the following and explains the assignment orally:

1-5 Jonas
6-10 Jonas' family unit
11-15 community as a whole

"What does *as a whole* mean?" she asks the class. One student gives a definition and Anne confirms that she is correct, repeating it so that all students are sure to hear. When someone asks if it is okay to change the form of the words, Anne raises her eyebrows and asks the class, "What does that mean?" Once assured that the class understands the question, she confirms that they can substitute one form of a word for another if they wish to do so.

"How can we apply the word *bankrupt* to Jonas?" a frowning student inquires. "Let's start by looking at the meaning," Anne responds. As she directs students to look up the definition of bankrupt in their dictionaries, she comments, "Ladies and gentlemen, this isn't meant to be easy. You'll have to think a little bit about it." Then, after directing a student to read the definition aloud, she asks, "Can you have a debt of something other than money?" A brief but spirited debate erupts, ending only when Anne confirms that it is possible to apply the word bankrupt to the character of Jonas. When a student begins to offer a suggestion to the class about how this might be accomplished, widespread protest emerges. The class rule is that no one can use an example that has been shared by someone else, and most students in the room prefer to rely upon their own resources.

* * *

As she introduces a math/science lesson to her yawning class one morning in mid May, Anne begins by drawing students' attention to two objectives she has written on the chalkboard:

1. Convert fat, carbs, protein from grams to calories.
2. Calculate % of calories that come from fat, carbs, and protein in certain foods.

"It helps me to focus," she explains later. "In class, there's so much going on. Writing the objectives for the lesson on the board keeps me from going off on a tangent. If there is a disruption, I can just look at the board and remind myself of where we were!"

* * *

On a chilly day in February, Anne selects a group of eight students to join her in a nearby classroom while her student teacher conducts a different lesson with the rest of the class. The group chats excitedly as they walk across the hall and take seats at four waiting tables, adjusting to their unexpected but welcome change in environment.

Opening with a discussion about a story recently read by the class, Anne writes on the chalkboard:

Comprehend: Response:

As she encourages students to recall events and themes from the story, she writes the following quote under the word *comprehend*:

"It said in the story."

"In science and social studies, we've explained a strategy that you can use before you actually read," Anne reminds the group. "I think this strategy is going to help us immensely with our reading extended responses." She writes in all capital letters on the chalkboard:

SQRRR

Reviewing the first step of the SQRRR process, she elicits answers from the group as she writes:

Skim/survey:
    Key words
    Titles
    Pictures

"What are we questioning?" she probes the group as she transitions to the second step of the SQRRR process. She writes:

Question

The students are silent, unsure. Distributing a brief, non-fiction reading passage about Wilma Rudolph to each student, she circulates among the group. "What do you see happening in the pictures?" she asks. "Who is Wilma Rudolph?" Calling on individuals, she uses their observations to formulate initial ideas about the article. "I think she's a runner," one student responds. "She's wearing a USA jersey, so she must be American," another student observes. "It looks like she competed in the Olympics," offers a third student. With a variety of ideas about the passage established, Anne writes the third, fourth, and fifth steps of the SQRRR process on the chalkboard:

Read
Review
Respond

Next, she reads the extended response question aloud: "How does Wilma show determination throughout her life? Use information from the story and your own ideas to support your answer." Looking around the classroom, she asks the group, "What does *determination* mean to you? Was there a time when someone in this class felt determined?" Hands fly upward and Anne calls on several students to share their stories. As they talk, she writes on the chalkboard:

Determination
      Persevering – never give up
      Believing in yourself
      Confidence – focused – work hard
      Mind set
      Work hard

"I'm looking at the question, and it says 'throughout her life'," Anne comments. "Why do you think that's important?" After discussing the phrase briefly, Anne directs the group to read the story of Wilma Rudolph silently. Twelve minutes later, after confirming that everyone has finished reading, she says, "Raise your hand if you were right!" She leads a brief discussion about students' ideas of determination before writing on the chalkboard:

How does Wilma show determination?

Anne encourages individuals to raise their hands and share examples from the story as she writes them down. A few minutes later, stopping to examine the list created by the group, she notes that there is a large gap between Wilma Rudolph's birth and the time that she won the Olympic race. Students curiously skim the article again to look for additional examples. As the discussion continues, Anne expands the list on the chalkboard, fitting in new information chronologically:

Shows determination
      Low birthrate: determined to survive

Anne: Creative, Caring, Respectful

Paralyzed: worked hard, never gave up
Set record in college by working hard
Tonsils removed: missed practice: worked hard
College: determined to get into Olympic Games
Not giving up and winning the race

With six examples listed, she pushes further by saying, "There is one more place where she was determined...right at the end." When a student discovers the last example, Anne adds it to the list:

Dropped the baton: closed the gap: she was
going to beat

"Folks, I have you gathered here today because on the last two reading responses you've done extremely well. But you've got to connect your answer to what?" she asks. "To the story!" the group responds. "Folks, you've got to connect your thoughts to the story," she reiterates. "Are examples from the story implicit or explicit?" she probes. "Explicit!" students remember.

"So tell me step by step what you need to do," Anne continues. As she calls on individuals to explain the process of answering an extended reading response question, she erases one area of the chalkboard to create more space, writing:

Skim/Survey
    Title
        Pictures
        Question
Read/Review
        Explicit examples – at least 3

"And then you're going to do what you already do so well with interpretation," she reminds them. "Add your own thoughts and experiences!" Smiling, she says, "You know what your assignment is going to be. I'd like you to use our last ten minutes to get started because you have all of this

33

on the board." Quickly and quietly, students begin writing an extended response to the story.

Several minutes later, Anne gently breaks the working silence that has settled over the room. "It's time to go back to the classroom," she tells the group. "Give it your best shot at home tonight," she encourages. "Get all of that interpretation in there!"

* * *

On a warm, breezy day in May, Anne points to a circle drawn on the overhead projector and asks, "How do I figure out how much is 30%?" A few students raise their hands, and Anne calls on one and then another, listening intently to each. In response to one student's suggestion, she writes the following on the overhead projector:

360 degrees
.30 x 3.6 = 1.08

"So that's one degree," she states to the class as she reviews her work. "Does that make sense?" Several students protest that one degree is a far cry from 30%.

"What if I told you that you have all the right numbers in the equation, but your answer doesn't make sense?" she asks the student whose directions she has followed. The class is all ears. Considering this information, several offer new suggestions, and Anne works a second problem on the overhead:

30 x 3.6 = 108

"Does that make more sense?" she asks the class. Many students agree that it does, but the skeptics in the room suggest another equation just to be sure. Anne works the following problem, calling on students to compute as she writes:

0.3 x 3.6 = 1.08

Anne: Creative, Caring, Respectful

Looking at the answer, many students are confused, and some are growing frustrated. After a brief discussion comparing the answers of the three different equations, Anne tells the class, "I'm going to write it the way you were shown to do it three months ago." She works the following problem on the overhead projector:

$$.30 \times 360 = 108$$

Comparing the fourth equation to the second one, Anne and the class conclude that either results in the correct answer. When Anne points out that 108 degrees make up 30% of the circle, one student exclaims, "I remember now!"

* * *

During the month of April, after hosting a guest speaker to present the pros and cons of animal testing, Anne assigns a persuasive essay requiring students to take a position for or against the use of animals to test human products. During the first week, students write a thesis statement and one reason to support it, followed by several supporting sentences that are based on the comments of the guest speaker as well as additional research they have conducted. Anne reads each student's beginning draft and responds with two questions, written on a Post it note which she photocopies so that she can remember what she asks. Students are required to gather additional information or rewrite their draft so that Anne's two questions are answered. Then, they must take their draft to a peer reader for feedback on meaning before additional revisions are made.

The following week, the same process is repeated when students are asked to write a second reason to support their thesis statement. Again, when Anne reads the drafts, she asks two questions using Post it notes, and this time the peer reader asks an additional question before revisions are made. At the beginning of the third week, Anne presents a mini lesson on writing a conclusion, and students complete the first draft of their essays. Then, she presents a second mini lesson to address three recurring problems in her students' writing: misspelling of homophones, misuse of contractions, and forgetting to use commas in compound sentences. Requiring students to proofread and make corrections to their drafts following the mini lesson, Anne also provides a skill sheet that outlines exactly what she will be grading when she reads students' final essays. Students complete their final drafts independently, as homework.

* * *

On a cold day shortly before Christmas break, Anne conducts a whole class lesson about characterization using the novel *Tuck Everlasting* by Natalie Babbitt. Introducing three types of characters, she writes the key ideas of the lesson on a medium-sized piece of chart paper taped to the chalkboard. Written on the chart paper are the terms *round character* and *flat character*. After explaining in some detail, Anne writes the definition of a flat character as a character that is not fully developed but carries out action.

"Who in this story would be a flat character?" she asks the class. When one student suggests the man in the yellow suit, she probes, "Do you think he was developed? Did the author give us a lot of information about what he was feeling and what he had been through?" The class is quiet, thinking. Fifteen seconds later, the room is still silent. As she waits for a response, Anne adjusts her approach. "I guess I'm not saying this correctly," she begins. "What subtle thing did the author do to let us know that the man in the yellow suit was always there?" Light bulbs go on around the classroom as students begin to understand. When someone finally articulates that the man in the yellow suit was present in every scene of the story, Anne answers excitedly, "That's it! He was only the man in the yellow suit. We didn't even know his name, but he was always there! The man in the yellow suit is a good example of a flat character!"

* * *

Distributing photocopies of a student-completed math extended response to a small group of students on a dreary January afternoon, Anne tells them that she has removed the writer's name from the paper and they should not try to guess whose it is. Also distributing a copy of the ISAT math extended response rubric, she asks, "How many of you looked at the rubric when you got your paper back? How many of you just looked at your grade?" Sheepishly, most students admit that they haven't spent much time looking closely at the state assessment tool. Thoroughly reviewing the three columns of the ISAT rubric, Anne reads some sections aloud and calls on individuals to read other sections for the group. "What does *labeling* mean?" she asks when they encounter the word on the rubric.

A short while later, after they have read and discussed all of the performance levels in the Mathematical Knowledge section, Anne writes on an 8.5 x 11 piece of paper:

math knowledge = the answer
one flight of stairs down

"Ladies and gentlemen, that's your math knowledge," she announces to the group. "Now, I'm a scorer in Chicago. I want to see that you know the steps of this math problem." She orally reads the second section of the rubric, Strategic Knowledge, before leading the group through a discussion of how they might find the answer. "That's strategic knowledge," she tells them after they reach agreement on the most appropriate plan for solving the math problem. "Now comes the hard part," she foreshadows. "Explain it. What is *it*?" she asks, transitioning to the third section of the ISAT rubric, Explanation.

Showing the group a visual of an extended response that she has been creating as she teaches, Anne asks for the first step in solving the math problem. No one answers. As the group studies the student-completed model, she observes, "This person looked at the first step of his work and wrote down what he did. What key word shows us that he explained what he did?" Patiently helping them examine the student-created response, she asks, "How will the scorer in Chicago know that he explained his work?" As students analyze the model and begin to understand what is required, Anne confirms their conclusion. "What and why. You need both," she tells them.

Briskly directing students' attention to the computation on their model, she asks, "What's missing?" Then, when someone points out that the last step was skipped, she probes, "Does this student have the correct answer?" A lively debate plays out within the group. Anne listens with interest as students state their opposing views before asking, "Where in his work is the answer?" When students look at the extended response but remain silent, she says, "Okay. Let's go back to the rubric." She reads questions from it, such as "Is the right answer given?", "Is the answer labeled?", "Are all steps included?" "Is the computation completely shown?" while students look at the model and answer yes or no. Together, they determine the model's rating according to the ISAT rubric. "What and why," Anne reminds them again. "What key word lets us know that he explained why?" she asks. "Because, because, because!" she reiterates after one student identifies the word for the group.

Holding up the student model and reviewing the sections where the answer, the computation, and the explanation must be written, Anne next holds up a blank form and reviews the three sections again. Passing back each student's recent attempt at a math extended response, she tells the group, "When you get back to your seats, work on these first."

Student Assessment and Instructional Planning

"A learning community is when students know they're here to learn and they're excited about it," Anne asserts. "You have to offer opportunities that cause students to buy into whatever you're trying to teach them. If they're not connected to what you're doing, learning is not going to take place as readily." Anne believes that while successful classroom instruction is primarily the responsibility of the teacher, learning is also highly dependent on student effort.

* * *

"I use textbooks to begin my planning and then as a reference," Anne shares. "I generate 90% of my worksheets myself because then I can focus on a specific goal and I know I'm getting the exact information I need, which is whether they know it or don't know it." Anne also creates most of her own assessments so that she is sure to measure the key objectives of what she teaches.

* * *

Anne designs instruction with a range of student ability levels in mind. She explains, "There's always going to be a population at each end that you have to consider when you design your lessons or you miss them, yet you can't put it beyond their reach all the time because you get so much frustration." She finds opportunities to differentiate students' learning experiences through creative projects where students can apply their skills and knowledge as it relates to the curriculum.

Examples during the 2004-2005 school year include the design, creation, and display of electrified shoebox-size haunted houses to apply the principles of light, written descriptions and visual representations of new characters that could be added to the story *Tuck Everlasting* to show an understanding of varying purposes for characterization, the design, creation, and testing of sound mufflers to soften the clamor of the bell outside Anne's classroom to apply the principles of sound, and data collection through guest speakers, interviews, field trips, and the Internet to complete open-ended research projects on topics such as animal testing and the history of Illinois government.

* * *

Anne works hard to create opportunities for students to creatively apply the curriculum. Her principal reports that when she visits Anne's classroom she sees students collaboratively involved in learning activities that frequently integrate several subject areas. When asked to describe the types of activities they have worked on in Anne's classroom during the school year, students Kevin and Corrie recall examples of open-ended, high interest projects. "Earlier in the year we did the CATCH Program", Kevin recalls. "We went online to www.nutritionfacts.com and studied the food at fast food restaurants. Then we made graphs and matched the fats to Crisco and sugar. And then we had a healthy snack buffet, and we also did a CATCH Program night where everybody came and we had a fifth grade booth where people could see how much fat and sugar they are taking into their bodies when they eat that kind of stuff."

Anne's student Corrie shares, "There's a big project coming up in a few months. It's called the Old State Capitol project where we reenact the events that happened around the time when the Old State Capitol was the real capitol, not the old one. We get to go to the Old State Capitol and do our work there, in the building where Lincoln had his law office." Corrie also recalls smaller projects that she has competed under Anne's direction. She shares, "We've been doing a lot of math and reading this year. We just read *The Giver*, and before that we read *Tuck Everlasting*. Right now we're reading historical fiction books, and I'm reading *The Diary of Margaret Ann Batty*. She was on the Titanic when it sank only she didn't die. After we read, sometimes we make posters, or tri-fold displays about the book we read. One time we had to dress up as the main character from our book, and sometimes we write or memorize poems. There are lots of different ways that we can tell about the books we read. I normally get pretty good grades on those, I think because I like doing them."

* * *

Anne shares that she relies on frequent assessments to plan for instruction on a day by day basis. "I'm not a person who would be successful turning in lesson plans on Friday for the coming week," she comments. "The night before, I have an idea of what I want to do, and I frame it out. I look at the papers I'm grading, and I base a lot of it on that. For example, my goal is here, but 90% of them don't understand it, so I'm going to have to extend what I'm doing a little longer, maybe for another day. It takes me hours to plan, and I've been doing this for 16 years!"

Anne: Creative, Caring, Respectful

* * *

Between December and March, Anne's students completed five reading extended response essays in preparation for the ISAT. Analyzing the class's scores following each round of preparation, Anne designed future instruction based on specific areas of weakness according to the ISAT rubric. For example, during one lesson Anne emphasized the difference between implicit and explicit information and the importance of including a balance of both types in the extended response essay. In another lesson, she guided students through a strategic process of skimming the passage for a general overview before reading it carefully and responding in writing.

Anne used a similar strategy to prepare her students for the state math assessment. Every other Friday from November to March, she devoted class time to preparing her students for the ISAT math extended response. Beginning with a combination of modeling and direct instruction during late fall, Anne began organizing students into competitive practice teams shortly after the New Year. Presenting the class with a math extended response question, each group of students was responsible for collaborating to solve the problem, show their work, and write an explanation of what they had done. After completing the three-part task within a predetermined time limit, each group presented their work using the overhead projector, and the class discussed, analyzed, and evaluated each response using the ISAT rubric. "By the end of the year, they were quite good at calculating each group's score," Anne recalls.

Based on the group scores, Anne focused subsequent instruction on the skill areas where students indicated the greatest need, frequently utilizing small group instruction so that she could tailor her approach based on students' common misconceptions, areas of weakness, and/or levels of performance.

Climate and Classroom Management
"First of all, I'd like to congratulate you on your comprehension," Anne tells a small group of students one

bleak February morning as she opens a writing lesson. "You all did very well on your last assignment," she compliments. Later during the same lesson, when a student in the front row points out that the word *weight* is misspelled on the chalkboard, Anne looks at the board before saying, "Thank you! You're right!" Upon finishing the day's lesson, she praises the group as they gather their things and move toward the door in transition back to their classroom. "You've been a good group today!" she tells them.

* * *

Anne comments, "A classroom has to be a place where students feel comfortable asking questions and accepting other people's answers. Respect is a big one with me." She models respect by doing "lots of little things" consistently and sincerely. In addition to complimenting her class on their strengths when opening a lesson, and thanking them for their time and attention when drawing a lesson to a close, Anne refers to the class as "ladies and gentlemen" and calls students by name during class discussions and in private conversations.

* * *

On a gray winter morning, a group of six students remains talkative even after Anne begins a discussion about Navajo Indians. "Let me know right now, do I need to get Post it Notes?" she asks the group. "No!" several respond as the room becomes quiet. "Thank you. I appreciate that," she replies before continuing. When the talking erupts again mid-lesson, she pauses a second time to caution two boys at the back table. "You told me that we wouldn't need the Post it Notes," she says sternly. While the boys become quiet for a short time, their covert chat again becomes apparent within five minutes. "Will you please run in and get the sticky notes?" Anne appeals to a student near the door. The boys quiet again as Anne continues teaching.

* * *

Anne's class arrives at 8:30 a.m. on an icy February morning, surrounded by the fresh scent of cold from the below freezing temperature outside. On the overhead projector, a message awaits the class:

Good morning! 2-24-05
Get settled!
Have homework (writing & math) on desk, ready to check.
Begin work on Math Review 22.

As the class calms and begins to work, Anne circulates around the classroom, one desk at a time. When she asks to check each student's writing homework for completion, individuals pull their assignments from large manila envelopes that they use to transport their homework between home and school. Kneeling down next to each student so that she can make eye contact, Anne asks, "Do you have your conclusion?" before responding and briefly conversing with each student. To one she says, "You did really well on Tuesday's math quiz. Congratulations!"

When she comes to a boy who has not completed his homework, she asks, "Where is your assignment notebook?" Abruptly, the student pushes his chair from his desk and defensively crosses the room to his book bag, shuffling through a mess of papers and returning with a dog-eared student planner almost a full minute later. "Did your mom sign it?" Anne asks him, flipping to the current page. Avoiding eye contact, the student shakes his head but does not answer. "That's your responsibility," she tells him sternly. The student says nothing. "Meet me downstairs at lunchtime," she directs before moving on to check the next student's work. Grumpily, the student slumps down in his seat, mumbling something under his breath once Anne is out of earshot.

A few minutes later, morning announcements are broadcast over Dickenson's PA system. When the announcements end, Anne asks how many students have finished the math assignment, allowing them two more minutes to work after viewing their nonverbal responses. She kneels down at one student's desk to explain supplementary angles. The class becomes very quiet, taking advantage of their last two minutes of work time. Anne continues to circulate and assist students as needed, kneeling down to eye level each time. "Please, on number four, do not use a protractor," she reminds the class at one point. "It says, 'Use what you know about triangles'," she adds. Several students look up as she speaks, quickly checking number four before returning to their assignments.

* * *

Posted on the chalkboard at the far end of the classroom in early December are several large pieces of chart paper. The papers are labeled "How to stop the talking/shouting out", "How to stop arguing", and "How to stop disrespect". While the first one includes a list of suggestions already completed by the class, the second two remain blank, as if the class has not yet brainstormed ideas. Because Anne had to deal with so many student behavior issues during the 2004-2005 school year, she tried many new approaches. "I had to change my way of thinking from 'I need to control them' to 'I need to teach them'," she reflects.

* * *

On a beautiful day in May, as students reluctantly settle into their desks following morning recess, Anne reminds her talkative class, "I believe we're working toward that 2:30 p.m. opportunity." This quiets students considerably. "Thank you," she responds. Giving directions and allowing a short amount of time for the class to retrieve materials from their desks, she promptly claps a pattern to which students respond with an echo clap. She glances around the room to ensure that students are ready to begin as she states, "All I need for the first part of this lesson is your ears and your eyes." She moves to the overhead projector and begins teaching.

* * *

Turning on the overhead projector as the school day draws to a close on a sunny December afternoon, Anne displays a transparency she has written in advance, reminding students of their homework for the evening:

Anne: Creative, Caring, Respectful

Science Test Friday - Chapter 4, Unit F
Quality re-dos for *Wordly Wise* 8E
Good luck at the Christmas Program tonight!

She directs several students to distribute graded papers, and the class becomes talkative as they begin to organize for dismissal. Five minutes before the final bell, Anne counts to four to get the class's attention before giving a brief explanation of one assignment she has returned. A few minutes later, students begin retrieving their coats and book bags from the cloak room, returning to their seats and placing their chairs on top of their desks as a final task before leaving. When the 3:00 p.m. bell rings, students begin exiting the classroom. While some hurry out, a few students take their time leaving. One stops to ask Anne a question while another lingers behind to give her a Christmas gift.

Persisting toward Professional Growth

Anne shares that she worked hard during the 2004-2005 school year to better understand her students. While this helped her to appropriately modify her instruction into smaller blocks of time and discrete steps, she acknowledges that it was at the expense of depth in student learning. "I'm always concerned about the one step I didn't take," she comments. Following the characterization lesson in mid December, she reflects on the amount of depth she was able to provide. "Maybe I should have allowed more discussion since so many questions came up as soon as I gave the assignment. However, you could hear the antsy-ness going on, and they were beginning to erupt into side conversations. That, to me, says, 'Okay, we sat as long as we could. We have listened as long as we can. We're at our limit', so you have to get them focused on the assignment."

"Often, I find myself thinking, 'Oh! I'm out of time! They're stopping!' I know I'm losing them, so I take off the five or ten minutes that might have made the difference in the amount of depth I could have provided. Time is vital to the success of anything we do. I usually try to break up instruction into ten minute sections, and the next day another ten minutes, and then add another piece the next day so that it flows. But sometimes, like today, when we've spent several days discussing all that an author has done, their interest is zero. It's, 'Ugh. We're still working on this'."

*　*　*

During the 2004-2005 school year, Anne had an extremely challenging student in her classroom. The student was very defensive, questioning every decision Anne made and frequently resisting her authority, especially when she addressed his disrespectful and inappropriate behavior. Early in the year, Anne believed that she could reform the student and assertively held him to high standards by giving consequences and sending him to the office when appropriate. When the student complained that Anne didn't understand him because he was African-American, she would respond, "Please help me to understand."

Over time, Anne came to realize that this student needed to be treated differently than others. She learned that sometimes, rather than confronting disruptions and giving major consequences, it was more effective to overlook misbehavior or to address it simply with a reminder or redirection. But after several weeks she observed that, with this approach, the student was getting away with too much.

When an African-American student teacher arrived in Anne's classroom at the beginning of the spring semester, she approached his misbehavior by establishing firm boundaries, clearly communicating consequences for misbehavior, and following through swiftly and consistently when misbehavior occurred. When Anne noticed this, she began asking questions so that she could learn from the student teacher, sometimes asking for advice before responding to the student herself.

The student's misbehavior continued throughout the school year; but because Anne remained open to the ideas of others and persisted in finding the right balance for dealing with him, she learned to more effectively respond by accommodating his needs when possible and consistently applying consequences when appropriate. Her principal believes that this was the most effective approach Anne could have taken under the circumstances.

Chapter 2 provides an overview of Anne, a creative, caring, and respectful teacher, during her year of National Board candidacy. With an understanding of Anne's teaching practices, guiding philosophies, and thought processes during her NBPTS certification year, we next turn to Barbara, a National Board candidate described as confident, student-centered, and firm.

3

Barbara: Confident, Student-centered, Firm

Like Anne, Barbara is also employed by Knollcrest School District 802. While the two teachers met as National Board candidates during their certification year, they do not know each other well since Dickenson Gifted School is located across the city from Cady Stanton.

Cady Stanton Elementary School, built in 2000, is located on the southwestern edge of Knollcrest. Sitting on a sizeable piece of property within a subdivision of upscale, contemporary homes, the school is an attractive one-story brick structure that houses students from kindergarten through fifth grade. Serving a student body of 520, Cady Stanton employs a certified staff of 32 teachers, 50% of whom hold a master's degree or higher. Although no teachers at Cady Stanton are currently National Board certified, Barbara and one other teacher are seeking NBPTS certification during the 2004-2005 school year.

While 64.9% of the students enrolled at Cady Stanton are white, 26.3% are black, and 9.8% are Hispanic, Asian/Pacific Islander, or Native American. In addition, 34.4% of the student body is eligible for free or reduced lunch according to federal guidelines, 17% receive special education services, and .4% receives services for Limited English Proficiency (LEP). The school's attendance rate averages 95.3%, with an annual mobility rate of 23.2%. In 2003 and 2004, 73% of students in grades three, four, and five met or exceeded standards on the Illinois Standards Achievement Test (ISAT).

Barbara's classroom is located at the end of a long, shiny corridor, around a corner, and along a short hallway that dead ends with two – for emergency use only – fire doors. A consortium of student writings, posters, and other recently completed projects claim the short hallway as the point where Barbara's classroom actually begins. A rectangular table and four chairs positioned along one wall further add to the instructional utility of the otherwise unused space.

Inside Barbara's classroom, student desks are arranged into four horizontal rows of seven desks each. Facing a dry erase board that spans the length of the spacious classroom, the desks are positioned with their sides touching except for a wide center aisle. "The classroom arrangement changes frequently from groups to rows to partners," Barbara shares. Her own desk is permanently located at the back of the room within an alcove the size of a small office, a unique design feature of the modern school in which she teaches.

Over the dry erase board, a series of large, hand-printed posters are displayed. One is entitled *Non-fiction Reading: Before I Read, While I Read, and After I Read* while another sports the heading *Strategies for Solving Words*. To the right, cabinets that flank the room's width have been converted into a word wall, alphabetically displaying correct spellings of words frequently used and confused by fourth graders. Each word is neatly handwritten in cursive. The letter F hosts the words *follow* and *form*, while H reminds students how to spell *hope*, *hundred*, and *honest*. After the word honest, Barbara has written the side note *(silent h)*. Below the cabinets, coat hooks and an elongated, boxy shelf hang low enough that even the shortest students can reach them.

Flanking a large, shaggy blue rug positioned in the back corner of the room, a plethora of trade books, organized by genre and author, fill two large bookcases. Nearby, several small baskets, also organized into categories, are overflowing with even more paperbacks. To the left, a medium-sized tree branch holding an abandoned beehive hangs from the ceiling near a window; and a second branch, similar in size, displays a woodpecker's hole. A large butterfly kite is affixed to the ceiling over the carpeted area, and a potted philodendron grows green and spring-like as it sprawls across the top of a bookcase under the window. A 32-inch TV/VCR/DVD player is mounted high on the wall at the back of the classroom.

The following narratives provide a distinctive illustration of Barbara, a confident, student-centered, and firm teacher, during her year of National Board candidacy.

Communication and Instructional Delivery

Near the carpeted corner of her classroom, which Barbara frequently uses for brief lessons and small group instruction, posters on narrative, expository, and persuasive writing hang prominently on the wall. Each poster begins with a brief definition, followed by a summarized description of focus, elaboration/support, organization, and integration for each of the three writing genres. When Barbara's student Katie is asked what important things Barbara looks for when she grades a piece of writing, Katie responds, "She looks for everything on that big piece of paper hanging in the classroom. When you write, you just make sure that you've done everything it says on that big piece of paper."

* * *

At 9:45 a.m. on a snowy February morning, Barbara announces, "Let's make our transition to writing workshop. I'd like to meet on the blue carpet today." The class gathers quietly, and within 20 seconds all are cross legged on the shaggy rug looking at Barbara, who is seated on an oversized exercise ball at one corner. Beginning by praising the class on their writing progress over the past several weeks, she adds with friendly sarcasm, "And I know that you've all been waiting to do persuasive writing!"

As good-natured groans erupt, Barbara smiles. After reminding students that they will be assessed on persuasive writing at the end of the third quarter, she notes the persuasive writing poster hanging nearby before asking the class to join her in reading the genre's definition aloud. "So you're trying to find reasons to get other people to think like you do," she summarizes, launching a class discussion about possible purposes and topics they might select.

"Many of you have strong opinions," she states, giving two examples of views that might be held by someone running for student council president. "Can you think of any other examples of opinions?" she asks. Students are silent but alert as they think; their interest piqued although they have not yet fully grasped the concept of persuasion. Waiting a moment longer and still not hearing any ideas from the class, Barbara asks, "How many of you would like a raise in your allowance?" Eyes widen and hands fly upward as students begin conversing amongst themselves. After allowing the group to verbally explore the topic for several seconds, Barbara promptly changes directions. "Maybe there is something I do in the classroom that you would like me to change," she suggests. A new wave of conversation erupts as students excitedly discuss their thoughts.

"So, do we get the idea of persuasive writing?" Barbara asks the class a few minutes later. When most students nod, she continues. "Okay. Here's what I want to do. I want to get back to a writing workshop model more than me directing your writing like I've been doing. Each day, we'll start with a mini lesson but then you can free write. I want it all to be persuasive for a while, though, at least for the next week. You can write on one topic or several topics as long as it's persuasive." As the class collectively begins to shift, Barbara suggests, "You might want to spend today listing some ideas," before signaling that students may return to their seats.

* * *

Reading aloud to the class on a dreary December morning, Barbara pauses to ask, "What is a *gesture*?" Puzzled, the class has difficulty articulating a definition, answering that it is an emotion, an idea, a movement. Listening to each response without responding verbally, Barbara thinks for a moment before demonstrating two examples of gestures in an attempt to communicate the

52

vocabulary word's meaning to the class. First pantomiming a person looking through a pair of binoculars, she next puts her arms straight out to her sides and pantomimes the movement of an airplane. Watching with interest, students immediately identify the two concepts she is representing through gestures. Then, tying in a second vocabulary word, Barbara encourages the class to mimic her. "Mimic me! Remember, *mimic* means to copy!" she tells the class enthusiastically. The class erupts into a roomful of airplanes and people looking through binoculars. Students grin at each other as they participate.

*   *   *

Outside Barbara's classroom in April, the walls are lined with trees and vines, transforming the hallway into a virtual rainforest. Barbara's student Lisa explains, "We decorated it with the other fourth grade classes. Our class made the big vines, and we made the snakes and the flowers too." She continues, "We're doing a play in reading called *The Great Kapock*. It's about this tree and this man wants to cut it down and then he falls asleep because it's such a big tree, and all the animals in the rainforest come up to him while he's sleeping and explain why cutting down the rainforest would harm the environment and the animals." She adds, "I'm the bird."

Lisa is very excited about the play. "We're going to perform it on Earth Day because it's about the earth," she elaborates. "Only fourth graders get to do *The Great Kapock*. Each fourth grade class is doing a separate play so everybody has a part," she explains. "If I have time today in reading, I'm going to blow up a picture of a Macaw and trace it. My friend, she's a Macaw. She has the same line as me; it's just that she's a different type of bird."

*   *   *

On a wintry morning just after Groundhog Day, Barbara's class is organized into groups of two to five students. In preparation for the upcoming ISAT science test, individuals are reading non-fiction books on a variety of science-related topics. As students read, they stop periodically to add to a letter each is writing to Barbara, three paragraphs that explain what they already know about the topic, what they hope to learn, and what they are actually learning as they read.

While most students work independently, Barbara circulates to support those who need more assistance. In particular, she frequently stops at a table near the back of the classroom where two girls are sitting together. One is reading a book called *Animal Tracks* while the other reads *Solar System*. "Did you learn anything on this page?" she asks one of the girls. "What did you learn?" she probes. Listening to the student's answer, she encourages her to write it down before moving away to check on the next group. After briefly surveying the rest of the room, Barbara re-approaches the same student, checking to see what she has written before asking the same question a second time. "What did you learn on this page? Write down what you learned," she reminds her, adding, "You don't have to worry about spelling on this. Just write down what you learned."

"You have ten minutes of your reading workshop time left!" Barbara announces to the class after looking at the clock. "Even if you're not finished with your book, tell me what you hope to learn by the time you finish," she urges before summarizing, "so I want your letter today, even if you aren't finished with the book!" Continuing to circulate, Barbara soon returns to the two girls. Looking at their work, she tells them, "What I'd like you to do now is stop reading and finish your letters. It's okay to tell me that you're not done reading yet. You can finish tomorrow."

Five minutes before the day's reading workshop is scheduled to end, Barbara checks back with the girls one more time. "I want you to look it over," she tells one of them after reading the letter she has written. "Make sure you put your date, a closing, sign it, all of the things you include in a good letter." A few minutes later, as she begins collecting letters from individuals around the classroom, she routinely asks, "Did you put your date? Did you remember the closing?" Some students take back their letters to add these requirements before resubmitting them.

Barbara: Confident, Student-centered, Firm

Barbara reflects later, "With the workshop model, I have to keep checking in with those students who don't seem to understand. It's a matter of making sure they're doing what they're supposed to be doing and understanding the content we're studying." Even with the students in her class who are of higher ability, Barbara closely monitors progress. "Sometimes they run through things so fast that they don't get to the depth of it," she comments. "With those students, I have to slow them down, keep them focused."

* * *

In February, students in Barbara's class measure their pulses after sitting, walking, marching, jogging, and running. Engaging in each physical activity for fifteen seconds, students measure their pulses for fifteen seconds before multiplying by four to determine the number of beats per minute. With this data, students graph their pulses following each physical activity and then answer questions such as: "What happens to your pulse rate when you increase your activity level?" and "Explain how exercise keeps your heart healthy." Then, based on their resting pulse rates, they compute the number of times their hearts beat per minute, hour, day, year, and over the course of a lifetime. To apply their learning, Barbara asks students to make a list of heart healthy physical activities to try during recess, and as a culminating activity students design colorful postage stamps that could be used to promote heart health.

* * *

Barbara encourages students to draw in their science journals as a means of processing new information. During a unit on living organisms, students illustrate a plant cell and an animal cell in their journals before coloring and labeling the major parts and describing the important functions of the two cell types. Later, when asked to write and illustrate five main ideas about living things, Lisa draws a small fish and a big fish to represent the concept that living things grow and develop; and Katie draws a big fish getting ready to eat three small fish to illustrate the concept that living things get energy by using or making food.

* * *

On a warm day in April, Barbara directs students' attention to several pages of data that the class has compiled in preparation for making a circle graph. "Of the twenty people surveyed, how many liked blue?" she asks, calling on one of several students whose arms are stretched enthusiastically toward the ceiling. Affirming the correct answer, she rephrases it into fraction form. "So 8/20 liked blue," she says.

"Which fraction chose green?" she continues, thanking the student who gives the answer. As she systematically asks similar questions for each of the color choices in the survey, she writes the following on the dry erase board:

Blue	8/20
Green	2/20
Pink	5/20
Purple	4/20
Orange	1/20

"If you know the fractions, you have the information you need to make a circle graph," she states after drawing a huge circle on the dry erase board. Then, asking the class how to divide the circle into sections proportionate to the survey results, she listens to several suggestions before deciding, "Let's try Jake's method of dividing it into fourths." As she moves back to the dry erase board, she adds, "We'll try it, but we're not sure if it's going to work."

Looking to Jake for guidance as she follows his directions at the dry erase board, Barbara divides one quarter of the circle in half and then in half again. The result is messy and inexact. "Well, that didn't work real well," Barbara comments as she eyes the confusion of lines on the board. "We're going to have to erase, but I like Jake's idea," she encourages. "I think he was on the right track. I like how he started with fourths because he's familiar with fourths."

Again dividing the circle into quarters, Barbara uses one quarter as a model for the class. "I'm going to divide each fourth into five wedges," she explains. "We want them to be close, but they don't have to be perfect." As she divides each quarter into five smaller sections to complete the graph on the board, students draw wedges on their own circle graphs at their desks. The room is quiet with concentration as they work.

"Now, how can we show the information from the survey?" Barbara inquires. Together, the class studies the large graph on the dry erase board before one student suggests that because eight people liked blue they should color eight wedges of the circle graph blue. Barbara shades eight wedges on the dry erase board as students do the same at their desks. Understanding how to proceed, students continue on to the next color, working intently to complete their individual graphs. Barbara circulates to help as needed, occasionally posing questions to everyone. "How many wedges are you going to color green?" she asks as students look at their data and continue to work independently.

"Do you have the right amount?" she questions a few seconds later. "It should add up to twenty," she reminds, continuing to circulate. As the first students finish, she states, "As I'm looking around the room, I notice that most of you put all of your blue together, all of your green together, et cetera. Why did you do that?" She calls on a student who responds that it makes the graph easier to read. Students continue working independently to complete their graphs, fully understanding what to do at this point.

As soon as the class is finished, Barbara transitions to the heart of the day's math lesson: interpretation of data. "Which color takes up about half the graph?" she asks. "Which color takes up about 1/4 of the graph?" The two students on whom she calls answer correctly. "This is something kind of new for us isn't it?" Barbara mentions.

On the board, she writes:

$$\text{Pink} \quad 5/5 = \underline{1}$$
$$20/5 = 4$$
$$\text{Purple} \quad 4/4 = \underline{1}$$
$$20/4 = 5$$

Commenting on the reduction of the purple fraction, she tells the class, "We can get it down to 1/5 but not 1/4". Students work at their desks to reduce each fraction on the graph to its lowest terms. It takes only a few minutes. When she notices that most students are finished, Barbara asks the class, "Can you explain what you did in words? There's some space at the bottom for you to write what you did to make the circle graph. Think back to the very beginning," she urges. Around the classroom, students examine their work as they think about what they did and begin to write.

* * *

"We've been reading *Chicken Soup for the Kid's Soul*," Katie shares in February. "Then, we took a really good idea of an experience we've had and wrote about it and let other people read it. I wrote about when my grandma and grandpa's dog died when I was in first grade, and yesterday we typed them in the computer lab. I called mine *Dead*."

"In writing, we've been doing poems," Lisa comments in April, "and we're going to make them into a book. We have to copy five poems out of a book of our choice, and we have to write down why we chose them. We also have to put down the author and write it exactly how it was in the book. Then, we have to write our own cinquain, haiku, and diamonte poems. We write a couple and then we choose the best ones for our final copy. My diamonte is called 'Moon and Sun'. At the end, we'll put it all in order, like with a table of contents, and draw pictures about each poem."

"I think my most effective lessons are those where children are interested in learning," Barbara comments. "Effective lessons have a purpose for learning, even if it is something that is driven by curriculum needs."

Student Assessment and Instructional Planning

Every morning, on the dry erase board, Barbara writes the day's schedule. Including a ten minute meeting at the beginning and the end of each day, Barbara lists the time that each subject will occur and makes note of assignments and special activities.

Barbara: Confident, Student-centered, Firm

"If you look ahead in your planners, we're going to have a test over Chapter 6 next week," she tells the class near the end of a school day in January. "In your planners, turn to next Tuesday, January 25th, and write 'Social Studies Test Chapter 6' so you know that it's coming up." She explains later, "I always try to give them a heads up on what we're doing and what our goals are. They need to know why we're doing something in order to buy into it, and sometimes we do things because we know we're going to be assessed on them."

*   *   *

Barbara believes that understanding multiple intelligences is a key consideration in teaching. "It is important that you include avenues that every child can learn from," she remarks. "You have to do a variety of things from reading to talking to doing. You just can't do one or another. And you have to include kinesthetic activities so that students can actually experience it." Barbara also believes that it is important to connect student learning to the real world. She comments, "If you don't relate it to a reason why they need to know it, they don't even want to learn it!"

*   *   *

During the 2003-2004 school year, when Barbara taught a combination class of fourth and fifth grade students, she first tried independent social studies packets to better differentiate instruction across the two grade levels. "The kids loved it," she recalls, "so I began to develop the idea further. After a while, the kids began begging for social studies over any of the core classes where I directed the learning. So as the year went on, I set up more and more things like the social studies packets so they could work at their own pace and level. I had done a little bit of this in the past, but I didn't really give it enough of a chance," she reflects. "I think you really have to go with a change in instruction for some time to see how well it will work."

"Some of my planning decisions come from what the kids are saying, and some of them come from me

59

recognizing that it's a good time to teach something," Barbara continues. "When we were reading *Stone Fox* in reading workshop, I really hadn't planned on doing any writing with it, but the students didn't like the way the story ended," she recalls. "They wanted to change it, so in writing workshop we spent time writing new endings. At the same time, students were talking about writing dialogue, which I had discouraged them from doing until I taught it later in the year," Barbara remembers. "But I realized that it was a good time to teach it because they were writing an ending to a story. So we spent some time learning how to write dialogue so they could apply it to what they were writing."

* * *

Student-centered goal setting is part of the project-based, workshop model that Barbara uses in her classroom. In social studies, she helps students set goals toward completion of their chapter-based social studies packets. "Everything students have to do is listed step by step at the outset," she explains. "At the beginning of each chapter, I help them set a long range goal such as, 'We'd like to finish this packet in three weeks'. Then, each day when we begin social studies, we talk about where they should be in their packet by the end of their work time that day. I watch them as they're working around the room, and I help them set individual goals by asking them where they think they will be by the end of the week. Some are ambitious, set their own goals, and have everything finished before the three weeks are up," she remarks. "Others, I have to push."

* * *

In writing workshop, Barbara establishes overall goals for the class, conducting small group instruction as needed to enrich and remediate. Because everyone works independently with differing levels of support, students are engaged at various stages of writing at any given point in time. Barbara plans instruction and monitors student progress through formal and informal conferences. In addition, she helps each student maintain a personal writing portfolio. She shares, "I keep a photocopy of everything students write. Sometimes I keep the copies and sometimes I send them home for parents to see."

As winter begins melting into spring, Katie's writing portfolio includes a first and second draft of a manuscript entitled *No Smoking in Restaurants*. The first draft consists of an introductory paragraph crossed out once and written differently on the lines below. Barbara has written, "Good beginning!" next to the introduction and then breaks the second paragraph into outline form:

Reason:
1. Pollutes the air
--fills the air with smoke
--people breathe that smoky air
--it can damage your lungs
2.

Using Barbara's outline as a model, Katie goes on to develop her second and third reasons, *stinky smell* and *unhealthy*, before writing a closing paragraph for her first draft. Two days later, Katie's second draft is a neatly written, five paragraph theme. Also archived in her writing portfolio, the second draft closely follows the structure and ideas organized in the first draft.

* * *

When Cady Stanton institutes a school-wide recycling program in January, Barbara incorporates the idea into her class's social studies curriculum. Becoming active recyclers both at home and at school, Barbara's students make and display attention-getting posters in the hallways of the school to encourage others to recycle as well. "You have to look for opportunities," Barbara explains. "The best units come from things that are happening right now in the world. I recognized that we were already studying about the Amazon and the forests of the northeast, so I used that as a place to connect to recycling."

*   *   *

For reading workshop, Barbara maintains an assessment notebook for each student that includes a checklist of the state reading standards and the district benchmarks for fourth grade. She uses the checklist to assign plusses or minuses according to each student's ability to comprehend text at their current reading level. In order to gather this information over the course of a grading period, Barbara uses a variety of written responses to assess students' comprehension. She shares, "I have students write letters to me about what they've been reading during reading workshop. In the letters, I'm looking for specific information. I don't tell them what to write to show their comprehension, but they reveal it by writing what they think about the reading and how well they support it with the text. I also assess comprehension through extended reading responses, where students have to answer a question about a specific reading; and every once in a while I'll just give them some questions to answer, old-fashioned type things that they might have to do on a test somewhere."

*   *   *

Influenced by her district's newly-adopted standards-based report card, Barbara assigns quarterly grades in accordance with individuals' current level of performance. "I try to think of where I would expect a fourth grader to be at this time of the year, and that's how I do my grading," she explains. "For instance, at the beginning of the year, I have one set of expectations for writing as opposed to what I would expect to see at the end of the year, so it changes as time goes on."

Climate and Classroom Management

On a frosty morning in early December, Barbara stands near her classroom door as students arrive, take off their coats, and empty their book bags. Amidst the semi-chaos typical of morning arrival, she moves to the front of the room, waiting patiently as students make the transition from home to school. On the dry erase board, she has written four math problems and a sentence in need of spelling and grammar correction. After a minute or so, she says, "Take out your folders. I need to see progress reports." A surge of activity renews itself throughout the classroom. Several students approach Barbara with questions, and she talks at length with two students before they return to their seats.

The class becomes quiet again, students working restlessly. "I'm looking for a row to get their point for morning folder and daily work!" Barbara announces. Checking attendance, she notes that one student is absent. After taking lunch orders, she asks, "Does anyone have anything that needs to go to the office...basketball forms, passes...?" A problem with missing basketball forms becomes evident when several students claim they never received one. Barbara sends a student to the office to photocopy ten more.

Moving back to the front of the room, she directs students to hold up their planners so she can check them for parent signatures. Then, while she checks in students' homework, the class continues to plug away at the work on the board. After the Pledge of Allegiance is recited over the school's PA system and the morning announcements conclude, Barbara says, "Let's get started on our corrections." Drawing a name from a can of Popsicle sticks, one student is selected to suggest a correction for the grammatically incorrect, misspelled sentence on the board.

* * *

Barbara's students return to the classroom at 1:45 p.m. following their afternoon recess on a spring-like January day. With outside temperatures striving to reach 40 degrees, the weather is mild for mid-winter in Knollcrest. Students enter the classroom with wide smiles, flushed faces, and windblown hair. Ready to escape the confinement of their desks almost as soon as they are seated, the class springs into motion when Barbara gives them the signal to find their work partners.

The class is a flurry of activity as students stake out various locations around the classroom to work on their social studies packets. Several approach Barbara to let her know they are finished, so she asks them to bring their textbooks and packets to the rug at the back of the classroom. "Are you joining us on the carpet?" she calls out to one student who continues to wander around even as the rest of the class settles into work mode. Barbara takes a cross legged seat on the floor among six students.

"Any questions about this?" she asks the group. When one student speaks up, she opens a social studies book to a map of the United States, holding it so that all six can see. She explains how to read the map and use it to answer the questions in the social studies packet. "We sometimes have to go back to other chapters and rely on things we've already learned," she instructs when a second student asks a question. Shifting her position on the floor, she asks, "What kinds of plants live in the Northeast?" Then, directing the small group to the first page of a social studies chapter, she explains that they can use the subject headings to find the information they are seeking about plant life.

Before releasing the group from the carpeted area, Barbara asks them to revisit pages in their packets where incorrect answers were revealed. Although she suggests that students work with the same partners they had collaborated with the day before, students in the group want to mix themselves up and work with new partners. "Okay," Barbara agrees, leaving them to check on other pairs of students working industriously around the room. She shares later that she understands the importance of ownership in a classroom that emphasizes active student learning. "When students work on projects, they have to work out their own system with their partner of how they're going to tackle the work," she explains.

*   *   *

A bulletin board at the far side of Barbara's classroom, near the windows, announces, "I can write about what I read!" Then, it states, "We read *Stone Fox* by John Reynolds Gardiner," followed by the statement, "We wrote a fictional narrative." About 20 student writings are stapled to the bulletin board, and it is clear that the work is in final form. Student handwriting is neat, and the narratives are written on special paper. The writings were photocopied for display prior to being graded, so no scores or teacher comments mar the pages. As a visitor stands close to the display, reading some of the writings, a student approaches to proudly point out his own writing as well as his best friend's.

* * *

"You practically never get bored because you always have something to do," Barbara's student Katie comments about her fourth grade class. "[Barbara] makes what we're doing fun. My teacher last year would just read and read and read and then we'd do our work, but [Barbara] lets us do our work together."

Barbara describes learning as a partnership between teacher and student. "You can't force learning," she states. "Children learn when they're ready to learn, but I also believe that they learn when you've found a way to teach them." Barbara values the social aspect of schooling as much as she does the academics. "Students get more practice when they do things independently or with a partner, and it's important that they learn to get along with others," she remarks.

* * *

As student pairs team up to address their social studies packets on a Wednesday afternoon, two girls decide on a spot near the carpeted area and take several minutes to decide how to fairly divide their work. Reaching an agreement, both begin scanning their social studies books to find information about plant life. While most students work at pushed-together desks, about a quarter of the class is sprawled on the floor and a few have taken seats at a table positioned at the back of the classroom. About 45 minutes into the hour-long work time, two boys on the blue carpet switch to writing workshop, satisfied that their social studies packets are complete. One reads a story he has recently written to the other, who listens intently.

*   *   *

One morning in February, as students engage in various reading workshop activities around the classroom, a restroom pass is handed off quietly from person to person as several students leave the room and return within a short time. "A lot of you are using the restroom this morning," Barbara notices aloud. "Remember, you only get to go one time before lunch, so plan wisely!"

"I never have any behavior referrals from Barbara's class," her principal comments, "and it doesn't matter what kind of children she has in class that year. She just handles them."

*   *   *

"Sit down, please, so that we can go through our mail," Barbara directs the class on a warm afternoon in January as she transitions students from social studies to dismissal. The day's mail includes a school newsletter, a donation form for the tsunami relief effort, an H&R Block tax refund incentive, and entry forms for a name-the-robot contest taking place at a local hospital. Pulling stacks of handouts from a large box one bundle at a time, she briefly explains the gist of each before naming a student to distribute it.

Professional Leadership and Lifelong Learning

"Barbara's instructional leadership on the fourth grade team is a huge strength," her principal shares. "Her peers see her working with kids in her classroom, and ask, 'Wow. What is it you're doing?' She influences others by modeling, and she's able to move strategies forward in our school that way."

Barbara also shares her ideas and experiences beyond the walls of the school. "She recently presented at a promising practice fair in downtown Knollcrest," her principal comments. "She took one of the strategies that she uses in her classroom, the independent learning packets for social studies. She developed the project in concert with the other two fourth grade teachers, but she was the one who stepped up and said, 'I'll go present that'. She's good at that."

Barbara: Confident, Student-centered, Firm

* * *

"Barbara is very much a part of our school's learning community," her principal states. "She never wants to sit back and be uninvolved. She is one who will always join the book studies and discussion groups even though I often think she already knows everything we're going to discuss. She's always willing to join, and she always has much to contribute." Barbara shares that she has always been interested in professional development, attending and presenting at local, state, and national conferences throughout her years in the teaching profession. "I never get tired of learning new things," she says.

"I've always believed in active learning, but I had to learn it by trying it," Barbara reflects on her transformation to a project-based, workshop model of instruction over the past five years. She considers the professional development sponsored by the Ball Foundation, which involved collaborative research and the eventual implementation of reading and writing workshop throughout classrooms at Cady Stanton, to be one of the most significant learning experiences of her career. She reflects, "It was that professional development, more than National Boards, that really moved me along. I finally found something that supports what I believe in."

Professional reading is a key means of learning for Barbara as well. "I read a lot, and I learn a lot from reading," she states. She also identifies the diverse classes she has been responsible for teaching over the years as motivating her to seek new and more effective instructional methods. "Barbara places a great deal of pride in the achievement of her students," her principal observes. "She values the fact that the kids in her classroom are learning, and she does what it takes to see that it happens."

We learn in Chapter 3 that Barbara is a teacher who can be described as confident, student-centered, and firm. With an understanding of her, and Anne's, teaching practices, guiding philosophies, and thought processes during the NBPTS certification year, we turn lastly to Jamie, a National Board candidate who is committed, rigorous, and fun.

4

Jamie: Committed, Rigorous, Fun

Saxon School District 66 serves students throughout Saxon County, Illinois. The district is centered within the city of Saxon, a community of 110, 000 that serves as home to several manufacturers and industries in addition to two universities, three hospitals, and a variety of social, cultural, and recreational centers.

Serving a population of 11, 417 students in grades kindergarten through 12, Saxon District 66 operates 20 schools over a 200 square mile radius. The district employs 729 full time teachers and other certified staff, 41.6% of whom hold a master's degree or higher. In addition, 14 teachers employed by the district are National Board certified.

Built in 1999, Cassatt Grade School (CGS) serves 546 kindergarten through fifth grade students. Located on the northeastern edge of Saxon, CGS is surrounded by cornfields and Midwestern prairie prime for residential development. Many of the upper middle class homes within view of the school were built around the same time that the school was being erected. The entire vicinity boasts of contemporary quality.

With a certified staff of 39, 54% of the teachers at CGS have a master's degree, but none are National Board certified. While 80.6% of the students enrolled at CGS are white, 13.9% are black, and 5.5% are Hispanic, Asian/Pacific Islander, or Native American. In addition, 13.6% of CGS students are eligible for free or reduced lunch according to federal guidelines, and 20% of students receive special education services, although less than 1% of students in the school receive services for Limited English Proficiency (LEP). The school's attendance rate averages 96.2%, with an annual mobility rate of 12%. In 2003 and 2004, 85.4% and 84.2% of students in grades 3, 4, and 5 met or exceeded standards on the Illinois Standards Achievement Test (ISAT).

One of four classrooms clustered around the small, fifth grade commons area of CGS, the floor space leading to Jamie's classroom is partially obstructed by a traveling cart of laptop computers and a large box of dictionaries. Almost forgotten, a piano sits patiently to one side, not far from Jamie's doorway. Inside the classroom, student desks are organized into six groups of four, and Jamie's desk is positioned diagonally along one wall, offering a view of the classroom from all angles. On it, a scented candle burns covertly, lending an air of domesticity to the room.

Cabinets, shelves, an extended countertop, and a sink claim the area behind Jamie's desk. While much of the space is overflowing with books and other teaching materials, M&M people of various colors and sizes remain on permanent display. The collection adds color and a sense of fun to the classroom. Two hamster cages, alive with movement, inhabit the countertop; and several stalks of celery soak in clear, plastic cups of water dyed various colors with food coloring. A beach ball with numbers written all over it waits on the countertop next to a half-eaten box of Nabisco saltine crackers.

Along the left wall, running the width of the classroom, three, thick rugs provide a soft surface. Two padded rocking chairs with matching ottomans sit atop one of the rugs, and three bean bags and a large floor pillow with arms are strewn haphazardly across the other two. All of the décor in this comfortable section of the classroom is coordinated in shades of forest green, and matching curtains hang above the two narrow windows nearby. Next to the carpeted area, several novels are organized into stacks on a table, and a class-made quilt is displayed on a rack near the windows, each student-painted block representing a science event from pioneer times.

Under the windows sit two new computers, and on a short bookcase near the carpeted area, an extra credit advertisement is on display, attracting students with the boldly printed question, "Who Wants Extra Credit?" Two options are presented: "Describe a major battle of the Revolutionary War. Describe events along with causes and outcomes," and "Create and conduct a survey. Create a stem and leaf plot with a graph of your choice. Make sure it's neat and complete." Both options end with the encouraging statement, "Worth up to 10 points!"

Similar to the descriptions of Anne and Barbara, the following vignettes capture glimpses of Jamie's teaching practices, guiding philosophies, and thought processes during her NBPTS certification year, rendering a vivid portrait of a committed, rigorous, and fun teacher during her year of National Board candidacy.

Communication and Instructional Delivery

"On a sparkling April morning, as students begin the transition from math to writing, Jamie explains the day's plan. "Today, we're going to be finishing up your Earth Day papers. I graded them last night," she tells the class. "You have a spelling grade and a writing grade." Giving individuals the option of either revising their Earth Day paper or working on their endangered species report, she learns that three students have already completed both assignments. When one asks if he can hand in his report early, Jamie smiles and responds, "I love early. Early is a beautiful thing!"

* * *

As freezing rain pelts against the classroom windows on a bitter morning in January, a student turns in a homework assignment that is only partially complete. When Jamie asks him about it he seems genuinely confused, claiming that he thought he had done all that was required. Jamie reviews the directions with him, and he resignedly sets aside his morning work to complete the homework assignment.

Moving to assist a neighboring student who is struggling with a math problem, Jamie slips quietly away when she thinks he is ready to proceed independently. But when the student calls out to her in frustration a minute later, she returns to his desk and stays with him until he has completed the equation.

*   *   *

On a chilly day in February, Jamie briefly reviews the characteristics of a simple sentence before asking the class to give an example of a compound sentence. On the dry erase board, she writes:

Compound
I like crackers, and so does Lizzie.
and, but, or

After calling on students to identify the subject and the predicate of the sentence, she swiftly moves on to the third type of sentence. "Remember," she foreshadows, "Half can go by itself, but the other half can't." She writes on the dry erase board:

Complex
If you're at my party, be sure to bring nachos.

Directing the class to view the sentence closely, Jamie asks students to identify the dependent clause. This is difficult for the class, which Jamie has anticipated.

After thoroughly reviewing the characteristics of a complex sentence, she turns on the overhead projector to display a numbered list of 12 handwritten sentences she has prepared in advance. The sentences are written about Jamie, her dogs, and students in the class. She reads the first sentence aloud and asks the class to identify the type of sentence. Taking a vote by asking students to raise their hands as she names each sentence type, she calls on one student to answer. "How do you know it's a simple sentence?" she asks the student, who responds by naming the sentence's characteristics.

Jamie: Committed, Rigorous, Fun

While the sentences are written in blue marker, Jamie uses a red marker to underline key indicators that help the class identify each sentence type as it is discussed. Later, students complete a worksheet that requires them to identify the three types of sentences independently.

* * *

Each day before students arrive, Jamie writes the day's agenda on the dry erase board. Then, as various subjects are completed, she crosses them off. Next to the day's agenda, on a laminated poster, hangs a summary of the day's homework assignments. At the end of each day, Jamie takes several minutes to review the assignments written on the homework poster to ensure that students copy each one into their assignment notebooks.

"We pretty much stick to the daily schedule so that students know what to expect," Jamie shares, "but sometimes we switch things around. For example, if it looks like it's going to be a longer lesson or something difficult or more important for them to know, I try to do it earlier in the day. That's the nice thing about teaching in a self-contained classroom: You can be a little more flexible."

* * *

"We did pretty well with reducing fractions last week," Jamie tells the class as she introduces the day's math lesson, "but we didn't do so well with adding and subtracting. We're going to practice some more today." As she leads the class through the process of subtracting mixed numbers, she makes up funny stories and uses interesting vocabulary as she spontaneously writes equations using the overhead projector.

"Nate has 10 1/2 bags of popcorn," she tells the class. "He's afraid his teacher is going to give him a bad grade, so he gives her 8 7/8 bags." She works the problem on an overhead transparency as students work it on notebook-sized dry erase boards at their desks. When Nate sees the answer to the story problem, he exclaims, "Oh no! She didn't leave me any!"

73

A short while later, as the class examines the equation 6 pints = 3/4 gallon, a student asks, "Could we say .75 for 3/4 gallon?" "Sure!" Jamie responds. "I like that because it shows me that you know they both mean the same thing!" As she writes the next practice problem, she says, "Let's be fancy. Let's write 1.25."

*　*　*

"Once a month my mom and dad visit us, and we do a cooking project," Jamie shares. "Our first one is homemade ice cream because they have to take a cup of heavy cream and a cup of milk to make a pint of ice cream. They put it in a quart bag along with the other ingredients, and then they put the quart bag in a gallon bag and pack it with ice. They swoosh it back and forth until it solidifies, and then they take it out and eat it. It's our first practice for using cups, pints, quarts, and gallons," Jamie explains. Her student Cathren recalls the ice cream project as one of the most enjoyable activities of the school year.

"In December, we did a fraction project where we made chocolate chip cookies and held a bake sale so that we could give the profits to charity," Jamie continues. "Each group had to double their recipe, and after they doubled all the fractions and converted them to mixed numbers, they made the cookies. They work in groups, and I always check their math before they go to the cooking area so that I know they've doubled the recipe correctly. Otherwise, we might not be selling anything!"

In addition to creative coverage of math curriculum, the intergenerational aspect of the cooking projects is an added bonus for Jamie's students. Her principal comments, "The class gets to know Jamie's parents, and her parents get to know the kids too. It's nice, especially for those who don't have grandparents living in the area."

*　*　*

On a cold morning in February, Jamie announces that the first of several students is ready to present the simple machine he has created. Reminding the class that there should be no talking, she gives the student a signal to begin.

Jamie: Committed, Rigorous, Fun

He displays a poster defining each of three types of levers, holding up examples of each type after identifying and describing their characteristics. The student shows the class an eyebrow clipper, a pair of needle nose pliers, and a pair of scissors, pointing out the location of the load, the force, and the fulcrum on each tool. Then, for the grand finale, he demonstrates the use of a lever with a teeter totter he has made with a 2 x 4 and a plastic storage tub. The class watches with a great deal of interest. Jamie also watches, listening carefully as she makes notes on an assessment rubric. When the presentation is complete, the class applauds enthusiastically.

After allowing a few minutes for set up, Jamie asks the second student presenter if she is ready. This student's project involves a model of a barn that uses a lever and pulley to transport small bales of straw from the loft to the ground. When Jamie asks the presenter what kind of lever is being used, the student is unsure. "What's in the middle?" Jamie prompts. "A fulcrum," the student responds. With this information, she remembers what she has learned about levers. "So it's a first class lever!" she answers.

By the end of the third presentation, most students have left their desks to gather closely around the presentation area at the front of the classroom. The fourth student presenter explains and demonstrates his machine, which is designed to water plants or pour a glass of water. The machine uses two levers, a pulley, and a wheel and axle. "That's awesome!" someone in the class comments as the student uses his machine to water the classroom philodendron. "That's pretty cool, isn't it?" Jamie affirms.

When the seventh student sets up another large, elaborate machine, most students move in even closer. Demonstrating a complex machine built out of tinker toys, the student uses a wheel and axle, a pulley, and two levers to cause a hammer to drop, cracking open a pistachio. The class is thrilled.

"I try to get students to show me what they've learned by putting things together and creating something new," shares Jamie. "They need to be able to find patterns and apply information to other situations."

*　*　*

Jamie frequently engages students in hands on science activities, called experiments. Before a science experiment begins, each student writes a statement of hypothesis to predict the outcome of the experiment. Then, upon completion, students list the materials they used and write a sequential account of the procedures they carried out. Finally, they describe the results of the experiment and draw conclusions about what they learned.

Jamie's student Cathren shares, "We do lots of experiments. Right now we're doing a celery experiment to see the xylem and the phloem. The phloem is how the plant gets its food because the food flows down the phloem, and the xylem is the part that carries the water and the minerals. We put food coloring and water together on the bottom so we could see how the xylem got all the leaves to turn that color, like the red food coloring turns the leaves orange on the celery. I understand it better when we actually do it."

"Kids are very tactile. They like to be doing something as opposed to listening," Jamie comments. "It's important to give them something that they'll remember, something to give them an experience, to click them, because ten years from now they are not going to remember any lesson I taught. What they will remember is what we did. They'll remember the experience, especially if it's something different."

*　*　*

Asking the class on a sunny morning in April to recall food preparation activities completed earlier in the school year, students enthusiastically share memories of making ice cream and baking cookies. "Someone put in one cup of baking powder instead of one teaspoon, but I'm not mentioning any names," Jamie teases as one student flushes and the rest of the class laughs. After allowing several students to reminisce, Jamie reminds the class that making ice cream and baking cookies are ways of practicing standard measurement for capacity. "Anybody know what *capacity* means?" she asks as she transitions to the day's math lesson.

Explaining that capacity is another word for quantity or how much of something, Jamie asks, "What are some standard units of measurement for capacity in cooking?" When students struggle to remember, Jamie refers them to individual "cheat sheets" that they created earlier in the school year.

Moving to the dry erase board at the front of the classroom, she produces a visual of the cheat sheet for those who can't locate their original copy. First, she draws a huge G, which symbolizes one gallon. Then, inside the G, she draws four capital Qs, one in each quarter, to represent that four quarts make one gallon. Next, to show that two pints equal one quart, she draws two capital Ps inside each Q, finally drawing two Cs next to each P to symbolize two cups in each pint. "How many of you like metric better?" Jamie asks when one student mentions liters. "How many of you like standard measurement better?" she balances.

About seven minutes into the lesson, the class becomes talkative and silly. "Put your foreheads on your desks," Jamie directs sternly. "Please leave your forehead down until you are absolutely certain that you are ready." The class quiets and Jamie turns on the overhead projector. Soon, they are ready to try again.

After leading students through several standard measurement conversions at the overhead projector, Jamie suddenly announces, "I need a board person! I need an eraser person! Light Boy!" The class springs into action. The lights flip on as one student distributes notebook-sized dry erase boards and a second follows behind giving out socks to be used as erasers. "Raise two hands: One for the board and one for the eraser," Jamie directs about three minutes later. Around the classroom, students confirm that they have the materials required for the next phase of the lesson as they hold up both items for her to see. "I like to keep things moving, so we transition pretty quickly," Jamie comments later.

* * *

"Raise your hand if you understood the directions," Jamie says after explaining how to do the day's grammar assignment one Wednesday morning. Most hands go up, but looking around the classroom she spots a student whose hand is not raised. She asks, "Do you have a question, Cody?" Nodding timidly, the student asks his question and Jamie answers it.

* * *

"There's a high level of engagement in Jamie's classroom," observes her principal. "Because of all the activity, there's a nice noise level in the room," he notes. "I really wouldn't expect them all to sit there stone faced and look at me," Jamie remarks. "I like them to get involved. Learning has to go beyond simple memorization."

Student Assessment and Instructional Planning

About instructional planning, Jamie summarizes, "First, you have to know what you want to get across to them, and then you need their attention. They need time to talk about it, to become familiar with it, and then you have to give them some practice and maybe a little independent work."

* * *

On a chilly morning in December, after Jamie announces that it is time for the class to take a timed math quiz, she concedes, "Okay, everybody groan at once," before counting, "One, two, three!" A collective groan reverberates throughout the classroom as she rolls her eyes with amusement and distributes the quiz. When Jamie says, "Begin!" a minute later, all but two students rush to complete a page filled with fraction reduction problems.

The two remaining students wait restlessly. One minute into the test, Jamie gives the signal and they dive in competitively while the rest of the class diligently continues. Later, while the day's math lesson is in progress, the two students quietly research the five senses on the classroom computers. One of them finds a colorful, detailed diagram of the human skeletal system and studies it carefully, making notes on a piece of paper sitting next to his keyboard.

Jamie: Committed, Rigorous, Fun

* * *

"I pick and choose from the textbooks," Jamie reflects about her instructional planning. There are some things that really aren't a requirement, so I skip over them. On the other hand, there might be concepts that we need more work on, so I add to those. It just depends on the goal I want to address. I have very high expectations for my students because I think that they all, to some degree, can master the fifth grade objectives."

* * *

Jamie's principal considers her one of the most flexible teachers at CGS in regard to adapting her classroom instruction to the frequent changes on the fifth grade ISAT. "She's wise enough to understand that she has to prepare her kids for ISAT, and she does it because she wants them to be successful," he remarks.

* * *

Jamie pretests students at the beginning of each chapter of the district-adopted math series. She explains, "Last week, we took a math pretest for an upcoming unit on integers, and I learned that several in the class sort of have the concept of negative numbers. A lot of them understand that -7 is less than 7, and some understand that -7 is less than -5, but nobody understands that -3 is less than -1/3. And when we try adding or subtracting with negative numbers, they don't get it at all. I've learned that we have a very, very basic understanding of negative numbers, so for our next unit in math we pretty much need to cover everything. It's good to know."

Jamie shares that her primary goal in math is to assure that every student understands the basic concepts in each chapter. To accommodate students of differing abilities, she provides occasional enrichment activities during class time and works with students who are struggling with the basics before, during, and after school.

* * *

When planning for instruction, Jamie admits that she doesn't follow the traditional teaching practice of writing the coming week's lesson plans on Friday. "If you looked in my lesson plan book, you would think I don't plan," she laughs. "I don't write a whole lot down, but I know where I want to go. I'll write down a topic, what the goal is, an assignment so that I can assess whether they get it or not, and any materials I need; but I change things a lot."

Instead, Jamie shares that she spends an ample amount of time organizing for instruction at the beginning of each week. "I usually spend Sunday preparing everything I'll need for the week and figuring out the specifics of what I want to do for each lesson," she explains. "I get my overhead transparencies ready and put them in order on the overhead cart, and I make photocopies and gather other materials I'll need. Then, I spend time thinking about my goals for each lesson."

* * *

While Jamie begins the planning process by considering the state learning standards, she quickly focuses on what she believes her students really need. Her strategy is to cover the standards generally and systematically throughout the course of the school year, slowing down to review, re-teach, or explore a topic in greater depth when appropriate.

"Students need to have a well rounded education," Jamie believes. "I try not to emphasize one subject over the others because they need a solid foundation in the basics." In addition to trying to spend relatively equal amounts of time on each subject area, Jamie frequently integrates subject matter to help students see the relationships between subjects.

* * *

On a windy day just before Christmas break, while teaching a lesson on subtracting mixed numbers, Jamie presents the class with a variety of story problems and works each one on the overhead projector while students work the problems on notebook-sized dry erase boards at their desks. As they finish, students hold up their work to show Jamie. She moves around the classroom, stopping to conference briefly with individuals as she circulates. Looking at one student's dry erase board, Jamie asks, "What'd you do? Tell me." Approaching another student, she asks, "Do you think that's right? You don't have to add?"

* * *

"We do a lot of homework," Jamie admits. "I monitor my students' progress every day. I check every paper and every little skill to see if they got it because I like to be on top of things. They do a little something in almost every subject every day so that I can make sure they understand."

Open ended summary is one means Jamie uses to assess student comprehension. *Five Very Important People*, in which students were asked to name five people instrumental in the westward expansion and explain how each person helped, is one example. Jamie's student Joe listed and described the contributions of Thomas Jefferson, Sacajawea, and Napoleon Bonaparte, along with two others.

Similarly, when students read short selections from supplementary reading materials such as *Scholastic News*, Jamie often requires them to write the correctly capitalized and punctuated title followed by a two to three sentence summary. One summary completed by Joe during the winter of 2005 reads:

"Journey to a Moon"
    A space probe is going to Titan. It is supposed to land January 14th. It has been orbiting Saturn since July.

Joe identifies the increased amount of homework as a significant difference between fourth and fifth grade. He states, "This year we have homework pretty much every night. I was kind of ready for it since I knew [Jamie] gave a lot of homework, but I didn't expect this much!"

Climate and Classroom Management

By 8:25 a.m. on a Monday morning, Jamie's fifth grade class is bustling with activity. Students enter wet and cold as a result of the sleet and snow mixture beginning to fall outside. On this bitter, January day, one to three inches of snow is expected. Excitement permeates the classroom as students take off their outerwear, hang up their belongings, and rustle through their book bags in preparation for the day. In the midst of the commotion, Jamie rings a small bell and asks students to take out their homework. Several call out questions, which Jamie answers in a friendly tone, but at 8:26 a.m., when she rings the bell a second time, she firmly directs, "Under control! Let's get to homework!" The class quiets considerably, but half are still standing, talking, and getting organized.

"Clap once. Clap twice," Jamie persists. Fully responding to her summons this time, the class claps in response and stops talking. All but two students have found their seats. Standing next to the dry erase homework poster, Jamie moves down the list subject by subject, giving the class directions about where to place each incoming homework assignment. "You had a logic problem to do," she reminds the class. "Put it in the center," she directs as students place it in the middle of their grouped desk arrangements. In addition to collecting five or six homework assignments, Jamie also collects book orders and report cards.

At 8:30 a.m., she says, "Okay. You should have all of your homework in nice, neat piles in the center. I'll come around and check them while you do your morning work." Jamie moves to her desk to take lunch count. "How many of you would like pizza today?" she inquires. "Raise your hands high!" She counts and enters the number online using one of the two computers at the back of the classroom.

* * *

During a spelling test in January, Jamie says, "Nicholas broke up with his girlfriend, so he is now *available*." Giggles erupt as students spell the word on their papers. "I'm teasing Nicholas because he is always talking about girls," Jamie explains, her eyes twinkling. Pleasantly embarrassed, Nicholas grins and shrugs.

"There's a lot of banter between Jamie and her students," her principal observes. "She jokes with them, and they feel a sense of belonging with her." Jamie's student Joe comments, "She makes it fun to be at school. We can do something totally boring, and somehow she'll make it fun. We get to do our homework at school, and we get to eat crackers in class when we get hungry."

* * *

On a bitter morning in February, when several students begin talking amongst themselves during a language arts lesson, Jamie warns, "I'm going to start giving checkmarks, folks. If I can make out your voice, you get a check." When some students begin whispering a few minutes later, she leaves the overhead projector to get her grade book. Knowing that this is the book where she records checkmarks, the class quiets immediately. "Sometimes with a class you can joke around with them and then make them snap right back, but this group has a real hard time doing that," Jamie admits.

* * *

Asking students to identify the subject and predicate of a sentence she has written on the dry erase board one winter morning, Jamie prompts, "We connect two simple sentences with a *what* and a *what* to make a compound sentence?"

"A comma and a conjunction!" several students respond in unison. Without warning, the class breaks into the song "Conjunction Junction", Jamie singing the first two lines along with them. When a student asks if they can listen to the song on CD, Jamie responds, "Maybe Friday," before refocusing the class on the day's language arts lesson.

Both Joe and Cathren note the fun atmosphere of Jamie's classroom. Cathren comments, "It's not just learn, learn, learn. We do lots of fun things like experiments in science and reenactments in social studies. I think the most fun I've ever had at school is in [Jamie's] class."

"We work hard but try to make learning fun," Jamie remarks. "We get along and enjoy our time together, and there's always something different to try. If I did the same thing over and over again, my students would be bored, and so would I!"

* * *

On a cold, wet February morning, after a student explains his Daily Oral Language (DOL) corrections to the class, Jamie comments, "You know, I think there are two things that still need to be corrected." The student re-examines the DOL sentence and finds one correction, but not the other. "Let me find you an assistant," Jamie offers, drawing a clothespin from a used Folgers coffee can that contains one clothespin for each student in the class.

Jamie asks the selected student to identify the final correction, but she cannot. Jamie draws another clothespin, but this student guesses incorrectly. "No, but good try!" Jamie encourages as she draws a third clothespin from the can. When another error remains undetected in the second DOL sentence, Jamie does not draw clothespins but instead selects two students to find the mistake by examining the sentence quietly while the rest of the class moves on to math.

* * *

Allowing students class time to begin creating Venn diagrams comparing and contrasting the American colonists with the British following a December social studies lesson, Jamie soon states, "Strike One already. I was going to give you the rest of the day to work, and you've already got Strike One." The class quiets, but one student disturbs the calm by tapping loudly and repeatedly on his desk. "When you do that, people can't work," Jamie tells him in a firm voice.

An atmosphere of silliness pervades the classroom. Although students remain quieter than before, several continue to chatter while the bold persist in fooling around. Two boys make rude noises near the overhead projector, and across the room three girls giggle uncontrollably. When someone belches loudly, all eyes seek to identify the culprit, distracting even those who are trying to work. Jamie gives a second strike before continuing to circulate and conference with individuals, but within five minutes, she says, "Strike Three! Maybe you'll get more time to work on social studies if you do a good job during math." Unsmiling, she directs the class to put away their social studies.

Commitment to Students and their Achievement

Jamie goes out of her way to support her students. At the end of the 2004-2005 school year, her principal shares two noteworthy examples. "Jamie had a young lady named Maddy this year whose home life is not very good," he recalls. "She struggled seriously with reading, and we eventually found that she qualified for special education services. Jamie spent a lot of extra time with Maddy. She had to find different materials and a different way to teach her to read. She even had to adapt her math lessons and spelling lists and the way she gave her science and social studies tests."

"Jamie did all of that, and over time Maddy started taking better care of herself. She started dressing up; she took some pride in her work. And at the end of the year, she came up to me with this huge smile on her face, and said, 'I'm going to junior high!' This was a kid that, when she came to us, got into trouble on the bus all the time. Then, the last two thirds of the year, not one bus report. Over time, Maddy began to believe that she could be successful in school, and I really attribute that to Jamie."

Similarly, when a South American student named Billy enrolled at CGS mid-year, his ability to communicate via the English language was extremely limited. Testing revealed that Billy qualified for Limited English Proficiency (LEP) services, but when his parents learned that he would no longer have Jamie as a teacher, they declined. Jamie rose to the challenge. As she had done with Maddy, she gathered appropriate materials, individualized her instructional approach, and spent a great deal of extra time helping Billy. "He would show up early and stay late," her principal recalls. "Jamie figured out how to help him, and it worked. Billy had a good semester here at CGS."

*   *   *

Jamie's principal shares that student achievement in her classroom typically ranks high in comparison with other teachers. "She pays a lot of attention to ISAT," he explains. "She also leads her colleagues in paying attention to the standards and assessments. They see her commitment and follow along. Jamie's grade level team works very well together in getting their kids ready for standards-based assessments."

*   *   *

Because Jamie prioritizes her students' learning above all else, much of her professional growth has occurred "on the job". She comments, "When you start out teaching, people tell you, 'Oh, it'll get easier. Once you have it down, you'll do the same things every year'. But I never do the same things every year. Everything's always new. There isn't much relationship between what I do now and what I did 20 years ago, and I think that's good."

Jamie's principal shares that she requests the gifted and learning disabled clusters because she enjoys modifying her instruction, assignments, and assessments in order to accommodate students across a wide range of ability levels. "She accepts challenges and seeks out ways that she can overcome them," he notes. "She doesn't shy away from having a behavior issue or a learning issue. In fact, she thrives!"

Occasionally, Jamie participates in learning opportunities outside of her school and district, but she does not draw attention to her efforts. "She is very private about how she's growing," comments her principal.

Chapter 4 reveals Jamie to be a teacher who is committed, rigorous, and fun. With an understanding of her teaching practices, guiding philosophies, and thought processes during her NBPTS certification year, paired with those of Anne and Barbara, we next compare the conditions, highlights, and challenges of each teacher's

National Board certification experience in order to fully establish a context for exploring teacher learning through National Board candidacy.

5

Reflecting on the
NBPTS Certification Experience

During the 2004-2005 school year, Anne, Barbara, and Jamie fulfilled requirements for NBPTS certification. Submitting their portfolios in March and completing the written assessment in May/June, the three teachers then waited five months before receiving their certification results in November.

To complete the personalized context helpful in exploring teacher learning through National Board candidacy, Chapter 5 exemplifies the conditions, highlights, and challenges of each teacher's NBPTS certification experience. In addition to openly sharing their feelings, perceptions, and insights about the certification process, each teacher's recollection concludes with whether or not National Board certification was accomplished.

Anne

"Seeking National Board certification is a personal challenge that people are either going to accept or they're going to say, 'Are you kidding me?' I've never experienced anything like it. Going through this process is a big gamble. The pass fail pressure is incredible. Not everyone is going to make it, and that's why it's so scary."

~ Anne, June 2005

Support during National Board Candidacy

During her certification year, Anne participated in a support group led by National Board certified teachers (NBCTs). While she loyally attended the bi-monthly meetings, she felt doubtful early in the process about the group's ability to help her. "Sometimes I show someone what I did, and they say, 'Well, this is what I did'," she comments in November. "It makes me think mine is wrong and theirs is right. Those meetings can be dangerous for me."

More helpful to Anne were the two fourth grade teachers at Dickenson who had recently earned National Board certification. In December, she shares, "They're right down the hall, and they look at me every day and say, 'We're here for you!' They've agreed to read my portfolio entries and let me borrow the books they found helpful, and they've even helped me with the technology."

She adds, "I don't have young children at home, and I have a husband who is 100% supportive. I couldn't do this without him. And my sister and my mom know not to call me on weekends right now, so they're in there pitching for me too. Without that, I don't know how a person could get through it."

But even with a wealth of support surrounding her, Anne observes, "I seek out things that I can do by myself. I have always been independent. I have a teaching partner, and I respect her to no end. But when I'm doing something really challenging, I want to do it by myself. I don't know why. It's just who I am. With something like National Board certification, you just can't experience it as a group."

Anne's Certification Year

"I think Anne had a good school year even though she was under a lot of stress," her principal reflects in June. "She had a very challenging class behaviorally, the most challenging class I've seen in 27 years. Plus, she was doing National Boards on top of it." Anne describes the quality of learning that occurred in her classroom during her certification year as minimal. "I'm not exaggerating," she insists. "Seventy-five percent of my day was spent with behavioral procedures, so I usually lost it before I reached any kind of depth. They just didn't have the maturity or the responsibility to apply it the way they could learn best."

Anne notes that she and her student teacher, who was assigned to Anne's classroom for the spring semester, had opposing teaching styles and behavioral expectations, which caused a great deal of tension for everyone. "I do not recommend taking on a student teacher during the NBPTS certification year," Anne firmly states in June. "You don't have as many opportunities to apply what you're learning because you want the classroom to be the student teacher's, so it ends up being more work rather than less."

Anne believes that, because she was working under challenging circumstances during her certification year, her portfolio entries may actually be stronger since she had to try a variety of approaches in order to achieve success. "She's very much a perfectionist," describes her principal. "Without the focus of the National Board standards, I think she would have felt like she wasn't achieving what she wanted to with this class."

Challenge of the Process

Anne felt that she had to modify her "way of being" in order to abide by the NBPTS portfolio requirements. "I had to reel in my creativity a bit," she reflects in June. "I'm in a school where creativity is encouraged, so my mind naturally goes way out there. The National Board is not 'out there' as much. It's pretty tight, pretty channeled." She was also frustrated by the strict parameters and vague guidelines for the NBPTS portfolio. "It's so open to interpretation," she comments in January. "Every time you read it, it looks like they're asking something different."

Wrestling with such challenges, Anne recalls working at home one Saturday in February. "I was going to spend a couple of hours sprucing up Entry 3, and I ended up spending ten hours fixing two pages! When I realized all the time I had spent, a frantic feeling came over me, and my mind started to block more and more. Finally, I put away the social studies and pulled out the science."

Conflicting Values

Anne feels strongly that the NBPTS is ignoring reality by not considering student behavior as a key aspect of the teaching context. "The one thing the National Board does not address is student discipline," she critiques. "They do not see it as part of being a qualified teacher, yet it stands in the way of being able to deliver curriculum, and it certainly affects how you teach."

She also questions teachers' ability to teach "the National Board way" throughout their certification year and beyond. "I think it's an excellent, excellent program, but I don't see how a person can teach well and complete the certification requirements at the same time," she comments in June. "It might have been the class I had this year, but teaching according to the NBPTS standards is totally consuming."

Even beyond her certification year, Anne is concerned with the amount of time it takes to teach "the National Board way". "It sounds so good when you read it, but it takes an amazing level of energy. I think you could realistically accomplish what they're asking two or three times a month because they want you to offer kids a wealth of information before doing the creative projects that I like to do. I understand that you can't just jump in and do a quick lesson because they need that background knowledge, but covering the curriculum slows you down. It encourages you to give depth to your teaching and it makes you aware of what you're not doing, but it slows you down."

Anne's Contingency Plans

"They told us going in that this is a three year process," Anne recalls in June, "but I don't know of anyone who wants to drag it out for three years. I went in thinking, 'I want to do it in a year', but now that I'm close to finishing, I have a different mindset. If I have to re-do it, I'll re-do it. I just hope it won't be every section."

Because she realizes the professional growth that occurred for her through National Board candidacy, Anne would like to make more of an effort to continue growing professionally in the future. "But I'm so tired," she shares at the end of the 2004-2005 school year. "I don't think I'll seek out new professional development, classes, or anything like that next year. I need a year to just not worry about it."

When asked in June to predict Anne's likelihood of earning National Board certification, her principal replies, "I think she'll get it. If she doesn't there's something wrong with the process!"

Anne's Certification Results

Anne learned in November 2005 that she had passed all requirements for both the portfolio and the written assessment, making her a National Board certified teacher (NBCT). "It was the most thrilling moment of my education career," she describes of the morning she checked online to find her certification results. "The relief was overwhelming. You tell people out loud that if you have to re-do parts you will, but inside you think, 'How will I ever muster up that momentum again?'"

Achieving National Board certification means a great deal to Anne because she earned it during a school year when she was working with a very difficult group of students. She reflects, "If I helped them at all because I was going through this process, then it was worth every minute."

Anne describes her NBPTS certification experience as a once-in-a-lifetime endeavor. She thinks that part of her success is due to the fact that she works in a school that expects and encourages creativity on a daily basis. In addition, she believes that much of her teaching was in alignment with the NBPTS before she embarked upon the process, making it easier for her to successfully complete the requirements. "If you aren't doing many of the standards already, you have a lot of work cut out for you," she cautions.

Anne will be eligible for retirement in four years. "I don't want to stop working because I love teaching," she shares, "but I'm hoping that being National Board certified will open some new doors for me." In the meantime, she looks forward to continuing in her role as a fifth grade gifted teacher at Dickenson.

Barbara

"NBPTS candidates are risk takers. Going for National Boards is a risky proposition."

~Barbara, January 2005

Support during National Board Candidacy

Like Anne, Barbara also participated in a NBCT-led support group that met every two weeks throughout her certification year. While the meetings were not mandatory, Barbara attended all of them. "It's very nice to go," she mentions in November. "You get good information, especially about using technology. But when they look at your portfolio entries, they don't really tell you whether you're on the right track or out in left field." One NBCT from the support group, along with a district colleague who recently earned NBPTS certification, agreed to serve as readers for Barbara, providing valuable feedback as she completed each of her four portfolio entries.

For additional support, Barbara frequently visited an online chat room for National Board candidates. "I'm getting these great hints," she reports in January. "I don't take everything people say as the gospel truth, but it makes me think. It makes me look things up if someone mentions something that piques my interest. The chat room has actually been a bigger help than my mentors," she reflects. "I can go online any time, and every time I've visited at least three or four people have been there chatting."

Barbara's principal also provided a great deal of support during her certification year. In addition to assigning Barbara a student teacher during both the fall and spring semesters, she was comfortable with Barbara working on the certification requirements during the school day when time allowed. "I'm very supportive of teachers who seek this certification," her principal states in January. "Any time you're taking a close look at your teaching and how you're connecting the curriculum to learning standards, it has to be a good thing. I look forward to having more National Board certified teachers in our district."

Barbara's Certification Year

Looking back on her certification year, Barbara comments in June that it probably was not her best year since she was consumed with completing the certification. "There were days when I was tending more to National Boards than I was to the academic needs of the children," she reflects, "but I think that's just part of National Boards. I don't think there's any way to get around that. In reading, I did more things as a whole group than I would have liked to, and I wasn't able to introduce new material like I typically do. It takes a lot of time to read all the books the children are reading, so I gravitated to old favorites. I also didn't do some of the larger, more creative projects that I normally do," she adds, "but overall, I had an excellent year. The kids learned a lot, and I was able to implement some really good stuff."

Challenge of the Process

"Last week, I was going to quit," Barbara reveals in January. "My computer had a virus, and it took me six days to get it fixed. The school's camera broke, so I have no camera to do the videotaping and I don't know when I'll have one. Because of that, I'm considering re-taping the social studies because it's on a tape that I can't access since the camera I taped it on is broken."

"My frustrations are not the professional development," she continues. "It's not the writing; it's not doing the lessons. It's the technology. My technology is breaking down all around me, and that's one of the reasons I was threatening to quit. And then, when I read in the NBPTS literature that I couldn't connect the writing and the social studies entries, I was ready to throw in the towel because I couldn't understand why one of my mentors didn't make that clear to me in the beginning."

"Those are the frustrating parts for me," she explains, "but every time I think about quitting, I think, 'I can't quit. I'm too invested in this'. I think the thing that helped me get my attitude back was staying up until 2:30 a.m. on Monday finishing up Entry 1. When I finished, I thought, 'Okay, I have two entries done. I can do this!'"

Beyond the technical difficulties, the greatest certification challenge for Barbara was adhering to the requirements of the NBPTS while remaining true to her personal beliefs about teaching and learning. She shares in early December, "I know what I'm doing is right. It's figuring out how to fit it in with the National Board's requirements that's so difficult."

But during the course of National Board candidacy, Barbara learned to trust her knowledge and experience over the advice of her mentors and the descriptions of accomplished teaching in the NBPTS literature. While she made some adjustments to her teaching practice during completion of her NBPTS portfolio, such as integrating math into science and administering teacher-led writing prompts for two different genres of writing within a short time period, she ultimately adhered to her established teaching practices. "I've learned to take advantage of what I already do and do well instead of trying to create a lesson that's not me," she reflects. "All of my portfolio entries ended up being what I normally do."

Barbara also feels that her decision to take the written assessment at the end of the school year was wise. "By completing the portfolio, you learn the National Board standards and you learn that you need to use rationale in making instructional decisions," she explains. "If you take the assessment too early, you might miss some of those things."

Conflicting Values

Like Anne, Barbara identifies unclear expectations as one of her greatest frustrations with the NBPTS certification process. She shares in February, "Sometimes I just wish they would spell out what they want. I know that we're supposed to just answer the questions, but they're still vague. It takes a lot of time trying to figure out what they're really looking for. They give you all this information, but they don't tell you exactly what they want. Most of the time, I feel like I'm guessing."

Barbara also questions the fit between the teaching practices promoted by the NBPTS and the policies of her school district. She explains, "The philosophy of the National

Board doesn't always align with what you're expected to do in your school setting. Even though the NBPTS is describing the way you should be teaching, it can be difficult to do. For example, I don't think the National Board supports the workshop approach to writing as much as it supports teacher-led writing. I believe in the workshop approach. At Cady Stanton, we go through a process with our writing. We teach narrative then expository then persuasive so the kids understand the different styles of writing, yet the NBPTS wants you to teach two styles within a three to four week time period which contradicts what I believe is good teaching. I somewhat see the value in doing it that way, exposing students to more writing styles and giving them more choices, yet it's very difficult to break away."

Barbara's Contingency Plans

In June, Barbara considers her chances of earning NBPTS certification. "After talking to people who have been through this process, I'm starting to realize that there's no shame in not making it the first time," she comments. "I found out that only 35% of the NBPTS candidates who tried for certification last year made it, so it's a one in three chance. Even the National Board says that it's a three year process, so to get it my first year is not as realistic as I thought it would be. If I don't make it, I'll just do whatever parts I need to again. It has to be easier the second time through because I won't be focusing on all of the sections." Even so, a short while later Barbara jokes half seriously about receiving her certification results: "If I don't make it, I'll cry!"

"You don't just get National Board certified," Barbara's principal points out. "You have to prove it. The certification really means something." She believes that Barbara's chances of earning the certification are outstanding.

Barbara's Certification Results

Barbara learned in November 2005 that she had achieved National Board certification. "I was thrilled that I earned it, yet I was really surprised at my scores," she reflects, explaining that she scored higher on portfolio entries and assessment responses that she felt were weak, and lower on sections she considered strong. "My scores show that there are some areas where I can continue to improve, yet I don't put a lot of faith in them since they don't match my opinions of my work," she remarks.

Barbara feels that, because she is an experienced teacher, her NBPTS certification scores do not reflect her learning during the certification process as much as they showcase her abilities as a teacher. She explains, "In order to earn National Board certification, you have to be able to use assessments to guide your teaching and make good instructional decisions based on those assessments. If I were a teacher with fewer years under my belt, maybe the portfolio entries would be more of a learning process because I would be questioning my teaching more. However, I was already doing a lot of the things the National Board expected, so for me it was showcasing what I already do. The challenge for me was trying to fit what I do into the NBPTS format."

"One of the biggest keys to passing is making sure that you focus on what you need to do to get students to learn, not on issues that prevent students from learning," Barbara says of the experience. "I don't think you can focus on problems when you're completing National Boards because the NBPTS is not there to solve your problems. You're there to solve your own problems by going through the process." She also believes that carefully planned writing is an important factor in earning the certification. "You have to focus on what you're doing and make sure that what you're doing will answer the questions the NBPTS is asking," she notes.

Barbara will be eligible to retire in fewer than ten years. "In the meantime," she comments, "I'd like to use my National Board certification as a springboard into something else. I'd love to mentor others or be a cohort leader," she shares. "I want to encourage others to seek the certification. Even though it's stressful and frustrating sometimes, it's worth doing." True to form, Barbara plans to keep growing professionally as she continues to positively influence both her students and her colleagues.

Jamie

"I don't think it was a bad experience. I'm glad I did it because it's a good activity for teachers to do. I just don't know if it really improves your teaching as much as you simply document your teaching."

~Jamie, June 2005

Support during National Board Candidacy

Due to the paltry number of NBPTS candidates in Saxon County during the 2004-2005 school year, no local graduate courses were offered to support teachers in their pursuit of National Board certification. As a result, Jamie enrolled in an independent study through a local university, along with one other teacher. "We get together with our professor/mentor and talk about what lessons we've done and what we're focusing on and what we're writing as we try to answer the specific questions for the portfolio entries," Jamie describes in November. "That helps me immensely. Otherwise, I wouldn't have anybody to bounce ideas off." In April, she recalls the assistance of her professor/mentor during the process of preparing her NBPTS portfolio for shipping. "She sat with us at my kitchen table one evening and helped us organize every single piece. She knows exactly how to do it. The directions were there, but without her guidance, it would have taken a lot longer."

In addition to the independent study, Jamie attended monthly support meetings offered by the Regional Office of Education. Although she attended faithfully, the meetings were not as helpful as she hoped they would be. She comments in November, "They make sure that we've covered everything, and they give us feedback on what we need to add, but they don't give us examples to look at. It would help me a lot to see what they're looking for."

Even with two formal support systems in place, Jamie's certification experience was overshadowed by isolation. "It would be much better if we had more of a support group because we'd have a little more feedback," she comments in December. She believes that her experience would have been easier if more teachers in close proximity were seeking the certification at the same time. "Especially in the same building," she emphasizes. "There is only one other person in the entire region who's seeking the certification besides me right now."

Even amidst low candidate numbers during her NBPTS certification year, Jamie considers herself fortunate to have the ongoing support of her husband. "That makes a big difference," she states in December. In addition, Jamie had a student teacher during the fall 2004 semester.

Jamie's Certification Year

Jamie considers the 2004-2005 school year to have been a good year, although she describes her students as less motivated than usual. "I would have had an easier time with last year's class," she remarks in June. Her principal agrees. "Jamie had a challenging group of kids this year, but her school years are always strong."

Describing her certification year as comparable to other years, Jamie comments, "I'm always trying to come up with a better way of doing things, but I didn't do anything extremely different this year because my main focus was on the NBPTS portfolio." Overall, Jamie expresses disappointment in the loneliness of the experience. She reflects in June, "If I could have shared ideas with more teachers going through the process, it would have been better."

Challenge of the Process

"I'm not sure it's worth it," Jamie says in January. "It's very stressful. I haven't done anything on the weekends for ages because I spend all day Saturday getting caught up on my school work, and then I spend all day Sunday either typing, revising, or analyzing videos, and if I have any time left I come to school and make sure I have everything ready for the week. That's pretty much my life right now. I want to do this as long as it doesn't take away from my regular job, but the moment it interferes with my job, it has to go."

Jamie identifies the genre of writing required for the NBPTS portfolio entries as one very challenging aspect of the process. "It's very different from the way I was taught to write," she reflects. "It's hard to break out of the way you've written for 30 years." She comments that the effort she put into the NBPTS writing genre took away from the reflective and analytical purposes of each portfolio entry. She also pinpoints the broad knowledge base required for Middle Childhood Generalist certification as a challenge. "It's impossible to be specialized," she comments. "When you're expected to know a little bit about everything, you often feel like you can't do anything really well because you have to spread yourself so thin."

As soon as school was out in May, Jamie spent three weeks intensely preparing for the written assessment. Reading professional books, studying social studies and science textbooks, and visiting recommended websites to review common misconceptions, miscue analysis, and other relevant information, she completed several timed practice essays through the NBPTS website and made up numerous others on her own. Following the written assessment, which she took in late June, Jamie comments, "The concentrated preparation gave me confidence and a wealth of content knowledge going in. It was not as terrible as I anticipated!"

Conflicting Values

Jamie doubts whether four portfolio entries and a timed assessment can adequately demonstrate a teacher's knowledge and skill. She believes that this makes it too easy for teachers to put on a show long enough to give the false impression that they teach "the National Board way" on a daily basis. Because she feels strongly that the purpose of National Board certification is to demonstrate accomplished teaching as opposed to adapting instruction to more closely align with the NBPTS philosophy, she believes that it would be unethical to showcase anything other than what she normally does in her classroom.

"The portfolio should represent what I normally do, and if it meets the qualifications, wonderful. But if I'm changing what I'm doing only long enough to earn the certification, then I shouldn't be doing it," she states emphatically. "I don't mind trying to videotape several lessons that I think will qualify," she continues, "but I'm not going to do one totally out of it lesson just because I think the National Board will like it. I don't think that's what they want to see."

Jamie also questions the limited timeframe for completing the NBPTS portfolio. "I wish the time element could have been extended a little," she comments. "It would make more sense to have a full school year instead of having to complete most of the entries toward the beginning of the year when you haven't had a lot of time to work with the students. You have to do all your samples and videotapes in the first semester when I would have preferred doing them right before the portfolio was due. It's in the second semester when you've had more of an impact on your students and you can really look at growth."

In addition, Jamie struggles with the NBPTS literature in regard to its vision of accomplished teaching. "If you read the portfolio guidelines, it sounds like there is one way to be a good teacher and candidates are supposed to show that they're doing that," she observes. "But I'm not sure there's only one way to be a good teacher." In June, Jamie also comments that the self-reflection emphasis of the National Board certification process was not as helpful to her as a collaborative sharing experience would have been. She reflects, "Documenting what I already do was okay, but I would have liked the whole experience more if I'd had a chance to see what other teachers do. Then, I think I would feel like I improved more."

Jamie is also skeptical of the National Board's ability to improve the overall field of education. She shares, "I really don't see how this process is supposed to improve education. I don't feel like I did anything differently other than all the videotapes, writing, and studying. Educationally, I'm not teaching my class any differently because of this. It's nice that it documents what you do, encourages you to try new things, and reinforces what you're already doing, but National Board candidates who do certain lessons just because they're required for the portfolio are probably going to go right back to what they did before; and teachers who are already doing those things probably aren't going to change a whole lot either. I just wonder how it will actually improve education overall."

"There are no guarantees," Jamie comments in regard to her chances of earning National Board certification. "Because it's government funded, I wouldn't be a bit surprised if it's cut from the state budget. When I compare the number of people who used to pass to the number of people who passed last year, it makes me think that maybe there's a quota. I'd like to think passing has to do with a teacher's performance on the portfolio entries and the assessment, but I'll bet it has more to do with the amount of money available."

Jamie's Contingency Plans

"I would be shocked if she's not successful," Jamie's principal comments when asked if he thinks she is likely to achieve National Board certification. Even so, Jamie shares mixed feelings about her chances of passing. "I wasn't happy with the portfolio that I sent in," she admits in April. "I know it wasn't my best work. If I could have come up with a little more time I could have done better," she reflects. "After talking to other candidates who went a totally different direction with their portfolio entries, I'm afraid that I might be way off base."

Following the written assessment in June, Jamie feels more hopeful about her chances of earning the certification, although she remains unsure about her portfolio submissions. "I may not be a good writer, but I'm a hard worker," she asserts positively. "I'll go back and re-do the entries as many times as I need to." However, she is concerned about the financial expense. "The re-do cost per portfolio entry is $350.00," she states in April. "That's rather steep, especially if you have multiple sections that score low. I just don't know if I can swing that."

Jamie's Certification Results

Jamie received notification in November 2005 that she did not achieve National Board certification. Though she shares that she did not really expect to pass the first year, she was very disappointed when no explanation of her scores was provided with her certification results. She comments, "I was astonished to learn that no specifics are given. If I, as a teacher, gave scores without explanations, parents and students would be upset, and justifiably so!"

She points out that, with no examples provided during the certification process and no feedback offered to support her final scores, it is difficult to know where her areas of weakness lie. "It all seems to be a guessing game," she remarks. "Since I am not sure exactly what I did wrong, I don't know how to correct my errors."

If Jamie decides to continue her pursuit of National Board certification, she will have to revise and re-submit all four portfolio entries. One option she is considering is the completion of two portfolio entries before the end of the 2005-2006 school year and two more the following school year. However, she is not sure that she wishes to continue seeking the certification. In addition to the financial expense of re-submitting all four portfolio entries, she is doubtful that completion of the NBPTS portfolio is a worthwhile method of professional development.

"I may just let it go," she shares in November 2005, shortly after receiving her certification results. "These projects simply didn't allow me to grow as I hoped they would." Jamie emphasizes the non-collaborative nature of the NBPTS portfolio completion as a key limitation of her professional growth. She is utterly disappointed with the experience.

Chapter 5 illustrates the conditions, highlights, and challenges of National Board candidacy as experienced by Anne, Barbara, and Jamie during the 2004-2005 school year. Coupled with descriptions of the teaching practices, guiding philosophies, and thought processes of the three teachers during their certification year, a personalized context for exploring teacher learning through National Board candidacy is established.

Beginning with an account of the learning reported by Anne, Barbara, and Jamie during their certification year, Part Two compares the three teachers' learning experiences to the findings of recently conducted studies on the topic before exploring the varying nature and degree of their learning in light of Jamie's difficult learning experience. Using the context established in Chapters 1 through 5 as a point of reference, the reader is encouraged to construct her own ideas about National Board candidacy and the learning that takes place for teachers through the process.

Part Two:
Exploring Teacher Learning

6

Teacher Learning through NBPTS Candidacy

Drawing upon the personalized context established in Part One, Chapter 6 launches an exploration of teacher learning as it occurs during National Board candidacy. Detailing Anne's, Barbara's, and Jamie's personal accounts of learning before synthesizing their experiences with other studies on the topic, the chapter describes five general outcomes of teacher learning that occur through the NBPTS certification experience.

Anne
"I really didn't understand the gist or get into the meat of it until probably November, and even a month before the portfolio was due the light bulbs were still coming on."
~Anne, November 2005

The Value of National Board Candidacy
Despite the fact that she had a very challenging class of students, Anne believes that the process of seeking NBPTS certification positively influenced the teaching and learning that occurred in her classroom during the 2004-2005 school year. "It kept me focused on what I needed to do to provide quality education under difficult circumstances," she explains. "It kept coming up and saying, 'We don't really care what you're going through. This is what you're expected to do in this profession'."

More than anything, Anne values the "lens" that the NBPTS literature provided for reflection and analysis. "It was difficult because it made you think about decisions you were making in your classroom instead of just showing up and saying, 'Okay, let's start on this chapter today'," she recalls. "Sometimes, I would read the descriptions of accomplished teaching and think, 'Whew! I'm doing this!' Other times, I would realize, 'I don't do that as often as I should'. It was a constant reminder that in a single day there are fifty million steps to being a teacher, and you better hit as many of them as you can!"

Anne further attributes much of her learning to the professional reading she completed while studying for the written assessment, noting that completion of the NBPTS portfolio required her to think specifically about her students and their learning while the focus of the written assessment required more general application of knowledge. Overall, Anne identifies four areas of learning that she experienced during National Board candidacy.

Focus on Student-centered Instructional Goals

During her NBPTS certification experience, Anne came to better understand the relationship between instructional goals and her students' needs. "Throughout the certification process, I've had to explain the characteristics and challenges of my students in order to justify my decisions," she reflects in May. "I know this class better, inside and out, than any class I've ever had. I used to go forward based only on my creative thoughts," she continues. "I'd say, 'This sounds like fun. I think I'll do this', but since I've been planning based on my students' needs, I find that they are much less frustrated, and so am I!"

Anne also learned to maintain unwavering focus on her instructional goals. "During class discussions, I used to ask questions that I would pull out of the air, but now I make a direct connection to the learning objectives," she explains. "Because of the National Boards, I realize that a teacher can be way out there asking questions while the objectives are forgotten. Then, when you assess, you don't understand why your students didn't get it."

In order to remember her objectives while teaching, Anne now writes them prominently on the chalkboard or provides another type of visual for the class to refer to during instruction. For example, prior to small group discussions following a science experiment in February, Anne gave each group a large-print list of vocabulary words. She recalls, "They used the vocabulary as they talked in small groups, and I used the words when I questioned them. I would have never thought of doing that before."

Wise Use of Instructional Time

Wise use of instructional time is a second area of learning for Anne as a result of National Board candidacy. During an October science unit about light, students in her classroom created electrified haunted houses out of shoe boxes to demonstrate the concepts of reflection, refraction, and diffraction. "The students loved it," Anne recalls, "but in the middle of the project I realized that it was too heavy on the creative part and too light on the science concepts. You have to be sure you're making use of every moment you have those kids in front of you," she summarizes, "and I learned to relate everything directly to my instructional goals in order to make the best use of time." The next science unit taught by Anne also culminated with a creative project, requiring students to design, build, and test sound mufflers. As a result of her learning, she closely aligned the project and its assessment with the unit's instructional goals while still maintaining a high level of open-ended creativity.

Adjusting to Student Needs and Interests

"Students learn in all different styles, and that has been the most difficult area for me this year," Anne remarks in January. "I realized through National Boards that I cannot force my style on these kids. I had to learn to adjust to them. My teaching is structured differently now, smaller steps, clearer and fewer directions, and more focus on learning objectives. It's convergent even though I'm a divergent thinker. The National Board has helped me to clarify the way I think."

Anne also reports that she now takes time to gather feedback from students at the conclusion of lessons and units before moving forward. She notes, "The National Board taught me to take the time to ask students, 'What caused you problems? What was confusing?' Hearing their input helps me with my own reflection. I no longer just close my folder and say, 'Okay, we'll do this again next year'. I look through it and ask, 'Did I assess my objectives? How did the kids feel about the steps? What was challenging and what wasn't? What made them think?'"

Assessing Student Learning

"I always thought I was doing a very good job of assessing student learning, but I was missing a lot, especially individual accountability during group work," Anne reflects in January. Recalling how she improved her assessment of student learning during the science unit about sound, she explains, "Students designed and built sound mufflers to soften the volume of the noisy bell that rings in the hallway outside of our classroom several times a day. As the final assessment, they tested their mufflers and evaluated them for effectiveness."

Because she was using the project for one of her NBPTS portfolio entries, Anne had to decide how she would know what students had learned about sound during the unit. She shares that she was able to ascertain learning by asking individuals to explain how and why they would change the design of their mufflers to improve their results. "They couldn't just say, 'I would add more newspaper'," Anne explains. "They had to explain how adding more newspaper would cause a change. Examining their choices was the only way I could know for sure if they had learned the important concepts about sound that we had been studying. Before, I might have just said, 'What would you have done differently? Well, that sounds great. Next!' I've learned that you have to make the assessment apply directly to the learning goal."

Anne identifies miscue analysis, diagnosis of specific student misconceptions, as the most significant student assessment strategy that she learned during National Board candidacy. "*Miscue Analysis Made Easy* by Sandra Wilde was the most important thing I read in preparation for the written assessment," she comments. "If a student doesn't know his math facts, it may have something to do with the way he thinks he should complete the process, or how he sees the numbers, or how he thinks he is supposed to write the answers. You have to diagnose the problem accurately before you can correct it." Anne states that the value of miscue analysis lies in discovering and correcting the mistaken concepts students have internalized. "That's what I'm really careful about now," she shares. "I ask myself, 'How am I going to teach this?' I don't just open the book and jump in."

Barbara

"With National Board certification, there's an element of open-ended creativity that allows you to go in the direction you want, and it applies to what you're doing right now in your classroom. It's not some separate project over here. It's the type of professional development I like, something that I'm in charge of, that I know I need to make myself a better teacher, and where I can read books and try different strategies as opposed to going to a meeting and sitting there quietly while everybody in the room is getting the same thing."

~ Barbara, January 2005

The Value of National Board Candidacy

Barbara is very pleased with the NBPTS certification process as a form of professional development. In particular, she identifies the model of accomplished teaching provided through the NBPTS literature as a valuable tool for self-reflection. "It's making me reflect so that I do the things I know are right, even when it's easier to do the older, simpler method," she comments in January.

Barbara's principal believes that the process of seeking NBPTS certification has motivated Barbara to expand her leadership role at Cady Stanton. She observes, "Barbara has always worked well with her peers, but she usually works independently. Now she is making an effort to be a leader at her grade level, and other teachers are beginning to ask about and try the things she's doing in her classroom."

Early in the certification process, Barbara felt that the experience was reinforcing her professional knowledge but not teaching her anything new. However, as she progressed, she came to recognize the experience as a meaningful form of learning. She reflects in June, "I was learning all along, but not in the way that I typically recognize professional development. It wasn't until I started studying for the written assessment that it began feeling like professional development to me."

While she considers preparation for the written assessment to be the aspect of the certification experience where she learned the most, Barbara found the reflection and analysis required for completion of the portfolio to be valuable as well. "With the portfolio, it was not so much trying new strategies as it was learning to reflect on what I'm already doing," she explains in February. "As I'm planning the portfolio entries, I'm reading, and when I'm reviewing what I've done and writing my analysis, I'm re-checking my professional books, making sure that my goals and objectives are matching up, and reviewing what to look for as I analyze my students' work. These are things that I wouldn't be doing if it wasn't required." In particular, Barbara identifies six examples of learning that occurred for her through National Board candidacy.

Integrating Math and Science

Recognizing the natural relationship between math and science was a significant area of learning for Barbara as she completed the NBPTS certification requirements. After seeing how well the two subjects fit together during the completion of Portfolio Entry 3, she shares in June that she plans to continue integrating the two subjects in future lessons and units.

Encouraging Learning through Conversation

Barbara has also increased the amount of conversation in her classroom as a result of her certification experience.

She explains, "The National Board wanted to see children communicating with each other more often, and I realized that I needed to be doing more of that. It supports their learning because they are either teaching somebody something or learning from someone else." Because the project-based workshop model was already well-established in her classroom, she reports that encouraging more conversation around content-related topics was easy to accomplish.

Increased Personal Use of Technology

In addition, Barbara identifies the use of technology as an area of learning through the NBPTS certification process. "I think technology is important, and the National Board really forced me to get more training and use technology more. I am definitely using more technology since completing my portfolio," she reports.

Increased Focus on Student Needs over Curriculum

Barbara also shares that over the past two years she has become much more focused on the needs and preferences of her students when making instructional decisions, observing that completion of the NBPTS portfolio affirmed this practice. She notes that she has changed from a focus on curriculum coverage to an emphasis on paying attention to students and their learning styles. "I think that's the biggest thing: Really knowing your students and doing what's best for them as opposed to getting through the curriculum," she shares in February.

Greater Understanding of Miscue Analysis

Moreover, Barbara considers the professional reading that she engaged in during her NBPTS certification year to have greatly contributed to her professional growth, especially in regard to her understanding of miscue analysis. Citing *Error Patterns in Computation* by Robert B. Ashlock as a key reading, she reflects, "I've never considered miscues in mathematics before. I've always looked to see the mistakes that students are making, but I've never really studied them to see what I needed to do to address their needs. In the past, I just graded their work and thought, 'They got it' or 'They didn't get it'. Now, I'm looking at what they didn't get and why they didn't get it. I'm asking myself, 'What mistakes are they making and what can I do to correct those misconceptions?'"

Altered Beliefs about Effective Writing Instruction

By far, Barbara's most significant area of learning during National Board candidacy involved a shift in her beliefs about effective writing instruction. Although it was against her better judgment, she followed the NBPTS requirements and taught two genres of writing within a four week time period in order to complete Portfolio Entry 1. "We were doing a fictional narrative that was connected to a reading we had completed about the book *Stone Fox* by John Reynolds Gardiner," she recalls. "At the same time, we were doing a social studies unit about westward expansion and traveling across the continent in a covered wagon, so students were writing in social studies as well. I was worried because we completed both writings within a really short amount of time, but as it turned out, their writing was really good."

Barbara allowed students to write within two different genres because it was required for Portfolio Entry 1, yet doing so went against her belief that students should be immersed in one genre for an extended time period. Adding to her uneasiness, she assigned writing topics instead of her usual practice of encouraging students to self-select topics since this was also required for completion of Portfolio Entry 1. When students were successful on both counts, Barbara experienced intellectual disequilibrium because her beliefs about effective writing instruction were challenged.

"I look at the writing they did and it's much better than when I just keep harping on process, style and all that," Barbara reflects in January. "I keep going back to the research that writers write best about things they know, but I learned through this experience that that's not always true. They wrote this great Chapter 11 for *Stone Fox*, and they'd only read the book one time so they weren't as familiar with it as they would have been with a life experience, yet they did a great job. So I'm seeing that they can write about other things. It doesn't have to be direct, personal experiences. They can get it. It was the same way with the covered wagon essay, so they do know enough to write about a topic that I assign. I guess the learning in class made it possible for them to do the writing. I'm thinking about changing some of my thinking because of this."

Jamie

"Like any endeavor, you go in with high expectations that you'll benefit enormously. I'm not saying that I didn't learn and grow. I just haven't found this to be as enlightening as I hoped."

~Jamie, December 2004

The Value of National Board Candidacy

Jamie's principal, who considers her to be one of the best teachers at CGS, is not convinced that she has much room left to grow professionally. When asked in June if he thinks the pursuit of National Board certification has changed her in any way, he responds, "I haven't seen it. A person like Jamie is such a driven individual already. I wouldn't expect this process to change her a whole lot."

While Jamie believes that she grew professionally during National Board candidacy, she has difficulty articulating her learning. "It didn't really improve my teaching like I thought it would," she reflects in June. She reports that she learned "little things" as a result of her certification experience, yet identifies no specific areas of growth.

At the same time, Jamie believes that the NBPTS certification experience influenced her positively. She anticipates that, in going about the business of planning, teaching, and assessing student progress during the new school year, she is likely to recall practices and philosophies emphasized by the NBPTS that may influence the professional decisions that she makes. However, comparing the time and effort that she invested to the learning outcomes that resulted, she wonders if the process is overrated. Given time to reflect, Jamie identifies three areas of learning that occurred for her during National Board candidacy.

Recognizing the Complexity of Teaching

First, Jamie credits the videotaping and analysis required for completion of the NBPTS portfolio in raising her awareness of the complexity of teaching. She reflects, "As I watched the videotapes for Entries 2 and 3, I had to analyze every comment students made. It makes you aware of all the decisions you're making and the feedback you're giving all the time, things that you usually don't even think twice about. Before, I would have just said, 'We did this assignment and this is what we were working on,' but there is so much more depth to teaching than that. Teachers do a lot more than they think they do."

Viewing Students as Individuals

In addition, Jamie identifies that the certification process increased her awareness of the individual needs of the students in her classroom. She comments, "Everybody's a little bit different, and until you really sit down and conference with students or examine their work, you don't always think of the differences."

Expanded Knowledge of Content and Pedagogy

"I liked studying for the written assessment," Jamie remarks. "I especially found it fun to review topics in social studies and science that I don't normally teach." In addition, after trying it during completion of the NBPTS portfolio, Jamie wishes to continue the integration of math, science, and technology. She explains, "We did a science lesson, and we tied in graphing and used the computer too. When we were finished, the kids asked, 'What are we doing for math today?' and I said, 'That was our math'. It seemed to go over well with the students since they felt like they didn't even have a math lesson, and I thought, 'I should do more of this.' It was also beneficial because it saved time, and I like anything that saves time! Integrating data analysis and graphics into science makes sense. It's in our district-adopted math series quite a bit, and I could skip some of the practice exercises and integrate it into our science experiments instead. To me, it's a small change, but it makes a lot more sense to do it that way."

Jamie also wants to integrate writing into other subject areas after trying it during her NBPTS certification experience. "The kids had fun tying some of their writing topics into what we were studying at that point, so maybe I'll do a little more of that next year," she shares.

Modification: The Most Common Type of Learning

"Teaching is not just about knowing things; it is about the use of knowledge – knowledge of learners and of learning, of schools and of subjects – in the service of helping students grow and develop. Consequently, NBPTS believes that the most valid teacher assessment processes engage candidates in the activities of teaching – activities that require the display and use of teaching knowledge and skill and that allow teachers the opportunity to explain and justify their actions."

~NBPTS, 2004, p. ix

Modification, defined as adjusting previously acquired skills, strategies, methods, information, or beliefs to more closely align with research-based teaching practices or descriptions of accomplished teaching in the NBPTS literature, was the most common type of learning that occurred for Anne, Barbara, and Jamie during National Board candidacy. Modifying existing teaching practices in response to professional development experiences such as National Board certification has been noted as the most common type of learning in at least two other studies as well.

Summarizing the learning that took place during the NBPTS certification experiences of ten teachers during the 1993-1994 school year, Chittenden and Jones remark, "Several described the assessment as 'affirming' or 'validating' what they believed, noting that it helped them become clearer about their philosophy, and more articulate regarding the assumptions that shaped their instruction. In essence, they were saying that there were no major changes in everyday practice, but rather important modifications in how they understood what they did and why" (1997, p. 14). Similarly, in his study of ten Michigan science teachers, Lustick saw little evidence of teachers actually changing their beliefs or teaching practices as a result of the NBPTS certification experience, although he notes that "certain details of their practice may have been 'tweaked' or 'adjusted' to be more in line with the standards of accomplished teaching" (2002, p. 18).

Anne's commitment to focusing instruction and assessments on clearly articulated learning goals is one example of modification. While she had always based instruction on learning goals and objectives, she realized during the process of NBPTS certification that she did not always clearly communicate or adhere consistently to those goals throughout a unit of study or even a single lesson. Once she became aware of this limitation, she developed several strategies for maintaining focus on instructional goals and found that it dramatically improved the clarity and direction of her teaching as well as the quality of her students' learning. Anne's learning experience in this regard is a common one. In a survey of 519 California NBCTs conducted in 2001, 65% named the ability to clearly articulate learning goals for students as one way the NBPTS certification process had improved their teaching (CFTL, 2002).

Applying Learning beyond National Board Candidacy

Ideally, modifications in teaching practice initiated during National Board candidacy are carried beyond the certification year. In the year following their NBPTS certification experiences, both Anne and Barbara share examples of learning that they have established as a part of their teaching repertoires.

Anne identifies careful consideration of her students' needs during instructional planning as a teaching practice she has adopted as a result of her certification experience. In preparation for the 2005-2006 school year, she outlined the major concepts for the instructional units that she wished to cover, but stopped short of planning the units completely.

"A teacher's manual offers the content, but unless you consider your kids' emotional, creative, and developmental stages and abilities, the best of lesson plans can be nonproductive," she explains. "Hopefully, I'll keep that in mind for the remainder of my teaching career."

In addition, Anne shares that she now checks students' prior knowledge before moving forward with instruction. One example is her systematic use of miscue analysis in math. Once a week, Anne provides each of her students with a notebook-sized dry erase board, a marker, and a copy of the local newspaper before writing math problems, one by one, on the classroom's dry erase board. Students work each problem on their individual dry erase boards, using any extra time to read the newspaper. "I do this on the day we have a classroom set of newspapers because some of them are so quick to finish the problems," she explains.

She circulates around the classroom, looks at students' completed problems, and questions individuals' problem solving processes when she notices an incorrect answer. "I just ask them to explain each step of the algorithm, and the step where they went wrong usually becomes apparent as they're explaining," she shares. "Before, I used to just look over their shoulders as we were working math problems, or I would sit at home with a pile of papers and try to figure out what they were doing wrong, so any assessment I accomplished was hit and miss. The most important thing I've learned is that when students are doing math problems incorrectly, it's not that they don't remember what to do, it's because they're thinking differently than they should be. That understanding has helped me a lot as a teacher."

Barbara notes that she has increased the quality and frequency of communication with the parents of her students as a result of her NBPTS certification experience. She explains, "The value of parent communications became very apparent to me during National Boards." She shares that when she learned that parents were having difficulty supporting their children in doing math homework, she began preparing and sending home informational handouts to keep parents updated about what their children were doing in math and provide step by step directions for the math problems students are expected to complete at home. "It's been well received," Barbara reports, "so I'm still working on that type of information in order to maintain positive contact with parents and support my students."

Uncultivated Areas of Teacher Learning

Although both Anne and Barbara report examples of teacher learning that they have carried with them beyond National Board candidacy, both acknowledge practices that they have not cultivated beyond their certification year.

Anne identifies professional reading and committee work as areas where she has relaxed since becoming National Board certified. "During my certification year, I was on more committees than ever before because I wanted Entry 4 to represent that I was at least interested," she explains. "But you have to be there before school and after school. It was just overwhelming." Anne reports that at the end of the school year, she gave up her seat on most of the committees she had joined. In addition, she shares that although she learned a great deal while reading professionally in preparation for the NBPTS written assessment, she has not continued the practice into the new school year. "There just isn't time to do it," she comments. Instead, Anne continues to focus on making improvements in her classroom. "That's how it was before I began the certification process," she observes. At least one other study reflects Anne's sentiments. Fifty-four percent of 2, 186 NBCTs surveyed nationwide in 2000 commented that although they would like to take on more of a leadership role within their school or district, they do not have the time available to do so (NBPTS, 2001c).

Moreover, while Barbara's NBPTS certification experience convinced her of the value of integrating math and science instruction, she reports that she has not continued the practice into the new school year. "I'm no longer teaching science," she explains. "I am in a team teaching situation this year, and since we're teaching different subjects we're not integrating as much as we have in the past. I don't disagree with the integration of math and science; it's just that we couldn't work it out with our teaming this year."

Both Anne and Barbara modified some of their professional practices in order to attain National Board certification, yet not all changes were cultivated during the subsequent school year. Neither teacher disagrees with the NBPTS in regard to the value of maintaining these practices. Rather, both teachers report that the reality of their lives prevents them from making the practices a priority.

General Outcomes of Teacher Learning

Synthesizing the learning reported by Anne, Barbara, and Jamie during National Board candidacy, five general outcomes of teacher learning emerge: orchestrating the whole of effective teaching, approaching the act of teaching with intentionality, increased respect for student individuality, ongoing engagement in professional inquiry and reflection, and an increased sense of professional duty. In comparison to previously conducted studies on teacher learning through National Board candidacy, these outcomes are similar in nature to the learning of most other teachers who have completed the process.

Orchestrating the Whole of Effective Teaching

Through the construction of her NBPTS portfolio entries, Jamie reports that her awareness of the complexity of teaching increased as she documented her teaching practices and provided rationale for the decisions she made. Anne also gained a clearer understanding of "the big picture" during National Board candidacy, learning how to better coordinate the many parts that make up the whole of effective teaching. Reflecting on her teaching practice prior to her certification experience, Anne shares, "I knew what I was supposed to be doing, but I didn't know the importance of making sure it was all connected. I didn't know how important it was to have everything in place as much as possible."

Anne's and Jamie's increased understanding and ability to orchestrate the whole of effective teaching is mirrored in at least three other studies. In a survey of 519 California

NBCTs, 78% reported that the National Board certification experience strengthened their teaching practice in regard to assessing student learning and articulating learning goals to students (CFTL, 2002). Similarly, Bohen (2001) identifies clearer focus on student outcomes as one important aspect of teacher learning reported by the 13 National Board candidates in her study.

Moreover, in their study of teacher learning as a result of the NBPTS certification process, Chittenden and Jones found that candidates developed greater awareness of the assumptions upon which they base their instructional decisions, allowing them to more critically evaluate and modify their teaching practice. These researchers write, "While specific modifications in instruction were sometimes noted, these were described as growing out of a larger sense of what they were doing" (1997, p. 15). Jamie's and Anne's learning during National Board candidacy reinforces this finding.

However, two studies document teachers' inability to see the positive influence of National Board certification beyond their own classrooms. In one study, only one of 25 teachers who had completed NBPTS certification requirements reported that the process had helped him "to see the big picture" (Tracz et al., 2005). Additionally, while teachers in a second study believed that their own students were benefiting from their increased teaching effectiveness as a result of NBPTS certification, they did not see significant benefits to their colleagues, schools, or school districts (CFTL, 2002). This finding is consistent with Jamie's skepticism about the ability of the NBPTS certification process to positively influence the field of teaching overall. For at least some teachers who experience National Board candidacy, it appears that the whole of effective teaching does not extend beyond the classroom.

Approaching the Act of Teaching with Intentionality

Approaching the act of teaching with intentionality, as opposed to approaching teaching intuitively, was a second key area of learning for Anne, Barbara, and Jamie during National Board candidacy. For these teachers, intentional teaching involves efficient use of instructional time and ongoing, formative assessments to guide instruction. Noted by all three teachers, wise use of instructional time is one important method of teaching with intentionality. Referred to as "saving time" by Jamie and "eliminating the fluff" by Anne, all three teachers either increased their awareness of its value or developed new strategies for using time more efficiently during their certification year.

Barbara's and Jamie's learning in regard to wise use of instructional time took the form of developing new time saving strategies such as integration of subject matter. As a result of their NBPTS portfolio completion, both teachers came to support the idea of integrating math and science instruction, and both adopted the practice of connecting writing instruction to other subject areas.

Although efficient use of instructional time is not prominent in the literature as a key area of learning during National Board candidacy, one study identifies subject area integration as a notable aspect of teacher learning during the certification experience. Eighteen teachers from four states who completed elementary literacy portfolios through the Teacher Assessment Project (TAP) at Stanford University reported assessment of students as the most significant change in their teaching, citing that as a result of the experience they were more likely to integrate the language arts into various subject areas and draw from a wider range of instructional options when planning lessons (Athanases, 1994).

An additional aspect of using instructional time wisely involves designing lessons, activities, and assessments in close alignment with instructional goals. Anne's learning in regard to this aspect of teaching intentionally is most notable. Moving beyond simple recognition of student differences to embrace the implementation of various strategies for identifying student preferences and addressing student misconceptions, Anne came to understand the importance of assessing student knowledge and skill prior to planning instruction. Additionally, she learned to clearly articulate and adhere to her goals during instruction. Having developed a sense of how the various elements of teaching make up the whole, Anne successfully transitioned from approaching the act of teaching intuitively to approaching teaching intentionally.

At least four studies identify teaching with intentionality as an important outcome of National Board candidacy. In a nationwide survey of teachers who had recently completed NBPTS certification requirements, 80% of respondents reported that the experience convinced them of the importance of integrating state learning standards into their daily teaching practice (NBPTS, 2001b). Similarly, ten National Board candidates in a second study reported that they were challenged to become less intuitive and more reflective and analytic when making instructional decisions and assessing their instructional effectiveness during the certification year (Chittenden & Jones, 1997). A third study found that ten science teachers who had experienced the NBPTS certification process were more likely to rely on data-based sources of information, as opposed to their perceptions, as evidence of student learning (Lustick, 2002); and a fourth study of 120 math and science candidates identified dynamic learning, the purposeful use of new information and skills to improve student learning experiences, as the type of teacher learning that occurs most often during National Board candidacy (Lustick & Sykes, 2006).

In addition to wise use of instructional time, teaching with intentionality also involves the use of ongoing, formative assessments to guide instruction. Both Anne and Barbara identify the use of ongoing, formative assessments as a teaching practice they improved upon as a result of their NBPTS certification experiences. While both share that they previously used assessments as one means of guiding instruction, both state that the NBPTS certification process convinced them to use ongoing, formative assessments routinely and as a primary source of direction. For both Anne and Barbara, reading about and engaging in the practice of miscue analysis was the greatest area of learning in regard to teaching intentionally through the use of ongoing, formative assessments.

At least four additional studies recognize expanded use of student assessments as a significant area of learning during National Board candidacy. Eighty-nine percent of National Board candidates surveyed nationwide in 2001 responded that they had improved their ability to evaluate student learning as a result of their certification experience (NBPTS, 2001b). Similarly, in a study of 25 teachers from California, Ohio, and Texas who had completed requirements for NBPTS certification, 76% believed that the process enhanced their ability to diagnose and evaluate their students' learning (Tracz et al., 2005).

In a third study, 12% of the teachers surveyed reported that they now use ongoing assessments to guide instruction more frequently than they did prior to National Board candidacy, and 24% reported that they have expanded the range of assessments that they use to gauge student progress. Further, after completing elementary literacy portfolios as part of the Teacher Assessment Project (TAP) at Stanford University, participating teachers reported that keeping detailed and varied records of students' literacy development caused them to focus more attention on individual student progress, which resulted in more frequent assessment and adjustment of their teaching (Athanases, 1994). At this time, no other studies specifically mention the strategy of miscue analysis as an area of teacher learning during National Board candidacy.

Increased Respect for Student Individuality

Ongoing, formative assessments allow for the intentional design and adaptation of instruction so that varying student needs can be accommodated. Their routine use as a guide for instruction is an important characteristic of teaching intentionally because it demonstrates respect for student individuality. Increased respect for student individuality is a third area of learning for Anne, Barbara, and Jamie during National Board candidacy. Beyond their increased use of ongoing, formative assessments, all three teachers demonstrate increased respect for students as individuals through instructional decisions aimed at meeting specific student needs.

Anne's increased respect for individual students shows itself through changes in teaching practices such as checking students' background knowledge prior to instruction, designing lessons and activities with students' learning styles in mind, and seeking feedback from students following instruction. One example is her intent to partially plan units of study for the new school year, completing each unit only after identifying students' prior knowledge, areas of interest, and related instructional needs. In addition, because she was working with a particularly challenging group of students during her NBPTS certification year, Anne learned to make accommodations for students based on behavioral needs as well.

Already adept at individualizing instruction through her well-established workshop model in reading, writing, and social studies, Barbara came to prioritize the needs of her students over straightforward coverage of the curriculum during National Board candidacy. One vivid example of this occurred when she consented to her students' desire to write different endings to the novel *Stone Fox* using dialogue. In addition, Barbara continued improving upon her student-centered instructional approach during her certification year with efforts such as encouraging more student conversation around content-related topics and expanding independent social studies packets into science.

Prior to National Board candidacy, Jamie was already adept at making accommodations for students identified as learning disabled, gifted, and Limited English Proficiency (LEP). However, she was less experienced at differentiating instruction for the wide range of academic abilities among the general population of students in her classroom. Through the process of analyzing individual student work during the completion of her NBPTS portfolio, Jamie developed greater awareness of the subtle nuances of student learning as well as the importance of taking those differences into account when planning instruction.

Anne's, Barbara's, and Jamie's increased respect for students as individuals is documented in at least three other studies. A survey of 519 California NBCTs found that 55% of respondents identified recognizing individual student differences as an improvement in their teaching practice as a result of their National Board certification experience (CFTL, 2002); and in a study of 25 NBCTs and former NBPTS candidates from California, Ohio, and Texas, 40% stated that they are now more aware of individual students (Tracz et al., 2005). Further, Mitchell (1998) elaborates that during National Board candidacy, teachers' methods of student assessment improve because they learn to closely monitor individual student progress and rely on evidence to ascertain student learning.

Ongoing Engagement in Professional Inquiry and Reflection

Anne, Barbara, and Jamie also learned to closely examine their teaching practices through professional inquiry and reflection during their year of NBPTS certification. As a result of National Board candidacy, all three teachers report that their thinking and teaching practices were modified to some degree through reading the NBPTS literature, "trying out" unfamiliar teaching practices, and analyzing their instructional decisions in writing.

Barbara and Jamie integrated math and science instruction and modified their thinking about teaching writing, while Anne developed several new strategies to maintain focus on instructional goals throughout lessons and units. Additionally, all three teachers enjoyed studying for the written assessment since they valued the new information gained through the process. In particular, Anne and Barbara learned a great deal about the practice of miscue analysis, and Jamie expanded her content knowledge in the subject areas of science and social studies.

Anne and Barbara note that the descriptions of accomplished teaching provided through the NBPTS literature served as a valuable tool for reflection during completion of the NBPTS portfolio. Both teachers share that they studied the descriptions closely, made frequent comparisons to their own teaching, and modified their teaching practices when they discovered a discrepancy and became convinced that "the National Board way" was more effective than their current teaching practice. One example is Barbara's effort to increase communication with parents in the year following her NBPTS certification experience.

Moreover, during their first year as NBCTs, both Anne and Barbara confirm that reflection has become an established teaching practice in their classrooms. While Anne reports that she learned the skill of reflection through National Board candidacy, Barbara states that the practice was part of her teaching repertoire before she sought the certification. Even so, both teachers report that they now spend more time diagnosing student needs, planning individualized instruction to provide for those needs, and analyzing their effectiveness afterward.

The vast majority of teachers who have experienced the NBPTS certification process report improved skills in self-reflection and analysis of their teaching practice (Bohen, 2001; CFTL, 2001; Chittenden & Jones, 1997; Lustick, 2002; Moseley & Rains, 2003; NBPTS, 2002; Sato, 2000; Tracz, et al., 1995; Tracz et al., 2005; Vandevoort et al., 2004). In a focus group discussion of 28 Indiana NBCTs, 37.5% identified professional reflection as a key element of increased teaching effectiveness as a result of the certification process (NBPTS, 2002); and 24% of 25 California, Ohio, and Texas teachers interviewed by Tracz and colleagues (2005) noted that since completing requirements for NBPTS certification they have become more reflective about the rationale behind their teaching decisions.

Like Anne and Barbara, teachers in a third study shared that showcasing their professional efforts and accomplishments through the NBPTS portfolio caused them to closely examine the value of each activity in light of the National Board standards (Chittenden & Jones, 1997). Similarly, one Oklahoma NBCT articulates that the NBPTS descriptions of accomplished teaching are such a powerful support to teacher learning during National Board candidacy because they provide a concrete, valid, and elevated means of comparison, which encourages reflective depth (Moseley & Rains, 2002).

Moreover, teachers in at least three studies credit the NBPTS certification experience, or similar experiences, with helping them to clarify their beliefs about teaching and learning. Teachers in two studies shared that the NBPTS certification experience enabled them to better articulate their personal teaching philosophies as well as the underlying assumptions and beliefs that influence their instructional decisions (Chittenden & Jones, 1997; Sato, 2000). Following the completion of literacy-based portfolios as a method of professional performance assessment, teachers in a third study reported that they were better able to articulate the reasoning behind their instructional decisions as a result of the experience (Athanases, 1994).

Interestingly, while Anne, Barbara, and Jamie each attribute a significant amount of learning to their preparation for the NBPTS written assessment, no studies identify the written assessment as the primary avenue of learning during National Board candidacy. While preparation for the written assessment provides a valuable opportunity for teachers to review subject area content, engage in professional reading, and apply their knowledge of teaching and learning to abstract, hypothetical situations, the absence of findings naming the written assessment as a key aspect of learning during the NBPTS certification process indicates that the majority of teacher learning takes place through the self-reflection and analysis required during portfolio completion.

Increased Sense of Professional Duty

A fifth and final outcome of National Board candidacy, reported by Anne and Barbara following their certification year, is an increased sense of professional duty. While both teachers recognize the prestige of being a National Board certified teacher (NBCT), Barbara's sense of duty takes the form of professional authority and leadership whereas Anne feels an increased sense of professional responsibility.

One of Barbara's motivations for pursuing National Board certification was to be perceived as having greater professional authority, especially in regard to decision making within her classroom. As a newly-certified NBCT, she believes that she has accomplished this. In addition to feeling more confident making instructional decisions that affect her students, Barbara reports in the year following

National Board candidacy that she has begun collaborating more with her grade level colleagues. Her principal notes that teachers at Cady Stanton now seek Barbara for guidance and new ideas more so than they did in the past.

Anne also notices the elevation of professional status since becoming a NBCT. Although she has not continued on most school-wide committees and has taken a break from professional reading in the year following National Board candidacy, she reports that within her classroom she has continued to place a great deal of time and energy on staying in close alignment with the National Board standards. She shares, "I feel this overwhelming responsibility to be the best teacher I can be. They handed this certification to me because they believe I'm qualified. Now, I'd better prove them right!"

Numerous studies examining outcomes of the NBPTS certification experience have identified increased self confidence and professional authority as results of National Board candidacy. Teachers in one study reported greater assertiveness and proactivity in dealing with the bureaucracy of education after completing literacy-based portfolios to document teaching performance (Athanases, 1994). In a second study, when asked to complete the statement, "Certification helped me in...", 519 California NBCTs responded most often with the statement "improving my self confidence as a teacher" (CFTL, 2002). Similarly, 91% of 2, 186 NBCTs from across the nation (NBPTS, 2001c) and 19% of 32 Indiana NBCTs (NBPTS, 2002) reported feeling more confident in their teaching abilities since becoming National Board certified.

Three additional studies have identified "perks" of becoming National Board certified that are closely related to increased professional authority. Ninety-two percent of NBCTs surveyed nationwide in 2000 believed that their NBCT status gives them more credibility within the profession of education, 90% reporting that they are considered a top educator in their school or district since earning NBPTS certification (NBPTS, 2001c). Similarly, in Kanter, Bergee, and Unrath's (2000) nationwide study exploring the potential value of aligning graduate art education courses with completion of NBPTS certification requirements, 69% of NBCT respondents reported that the most significant rewards in achieving National Board certification were their affirmed teaching practices, improved self-esteem, and increased credibility among their peers. In a third study, 13 National Board candidates noted greater commitment to professional growth and increased prestige throughout the community as two positive influences of the certification process (Bohen, 2002).

Further, at least three studies identify increased teacher leadership as a beneficial outcome of National Board candidacy. In a survey of 32 NBCTs from Indiana, 62.5% were offered leadership roles in their schools or districts after becoming National Board certified (NBPTS, 2002); and slightly over half of the 25 teachers in another study reported that becoming National Board certified had propelled them into one or more leadership positions (Tracz et al., 2005). Additionally, in a survey commissioned by the NBPTS that closely explored the outcome of teacher leadership through National Board candidacy, 2, 186 NBCTs who earned the certification prior to November 2000 revealed that 99.6% were involved in at least one leadership activity since becoming National Board certified (NBPTS, 2001c). Eighty-seven percent of these teachers also shared that fellow educators now seek their leadership (NBPTS, 2001c). Whether it takes the form of professional authority, self confidence, or educational leadership, many teachers besides Anne and Barbara have experienced an increased sense of professional duty as a result of National Board candidacy.

After detailing each teacher's personal account of learning as it occurred during the NBPTS certification year, Chapter 6 synthesizes Anne's, Barbara's, and Jamie's learning experiences and compares them to the findings of recently conducted studies on the topic. Identifying modification as the most common type of teacher learning during National Board candidacy, the chapter describes five general outcomes of teacher learning as a result of the NBPTS certification experience: orchestrating the whole of effective teaching, approaching the act of teaching with intentionality, increased respect for student individuality, ongoing engagement in professional inquiry and reflection, and an increased sense of professional duty.

Although Anne, Barbara, and Jamie share commonalities in their learning during National Board candidacy, several notable differences exist. Chapter 7 explores the varying nature and degree of learning experienced by the three teachers during their certification year and closely examines Jamie's difficult learning experience.

7

Jamie's Tenuous Learning Experience

"No two teachers reaped the same learnings from the process. Each teacher took away something different."

~Sato, 2000, p. 19

Of the three teachers, Anne reports the most learning as a result of National Board candidacy. Reflecting that she learned mainly through completion of the NBPTS portfolio, she comments that the process taught her how to integrate professional skill and knowledge toward greater teaching effectiveness. Sharing that as a newly-certified NBCT she feels an obligation to realize the National Board vision, she now carries a copy of the NBPTS standards in her plan book. "They're very helpful in planning units, and I continue to refer to them often," she remarks.

Barbara also reports learning through the process of National Board candidacy, but because her teaching practice closely aligned to the NBPTS standards prior to beginning her certification experience, she did not learn as much as Anne. Barbara's greatest challenge was adhering to the requirements of the National Board while remaining true to her personal beliefs about teaching and learning. Although she made some adjustments to her teaching practices to abide by the certification requirements, she reports that she most trusted her own professional knowledge and experience throughout the process. "I've learned to take advantage of what I already do well instead of trying to create a lesson that's not me," she shares in April. "All of my portfolio entries ended up being what I normally do."

Both Anne and Barbara applaud the fact that the process of NBPTS portfolio completion requires active engagement in research-based, professional improvement while also allowing teachers to customize their learning through application within their own classrooms. Anne remarks, "There are so many divergent ways to go with National Board certification. Even though they have rubrics for candidates to follow, you can still bring in your own creativity." While Anne embraced the NBPTS literature wholeheartedly, Barbara was more cautious, trusting her established professional practices until she had tried an NBPTS recommendation and found evidence that it was effective.

Jamie's professional growth experience during National Board candidacy was very different from Anne's and Barbara's. Harboring doubts regarding the validity of the certification requirements, she questioned the reliability of the process in identifying accomplished teaching through four portfolio entries and one timed assessment. Although she shared that she typically seeks professional development that offers an opportunity to apply new ideas in her classroom, Jamie felt strongly that the purpose of the NBPTS portfolio is to demonstrate accomplished teaching. For this reason, she resisted showcasing new, NBPTS-endorsed teaching practices in her portfolio entries because she believed it to be dishonest. Jamie does not feel that she learned much or significantly improved her teaching practice as a result of National Board candidacy.

The vast majority of teachers who have completed the NBPTS certification requirements report learning through the experience (Bohen, 2001; CFTL, 2001; Kanter et al., 2000; Keiffer-Barone et al., 1999; Linquanti & Peterson, 2001; Moseley & Rains, 2003; NBPTS, 2001a; Rotberg et al., 2000; & Thornton, 2001). However, while general outcomes of teacher learning have been identified, the nature and degree of learning as a result of the certification experience varies significantly from individual to individual.

In their study of 120 NBPTS science candidates, Lustick and Sykes identify three types of teacher learning during National Board candidacy. *Dynamic learning*, experienced by about half of all NBPTS candidates, is described as "immediate, meaningful change in a teacher's beliefs, understandings, and actions in the classroom" (2006, p. 25). Teachers who experience dynamic learning consciously and deliberately act to improve their students' learning experiences. Anne's learning during National Board candidacy is an example of dynamic learning.

Technical learning, which occurs when a teacher acquires techniques or strategies in order to obtain NBPTS certification but does not necessarily continue the practices beyond the certification year, is experienced by about 25% of NBPTS candidates (Lustick & Sykes, 2006). Technical learning best describes Barbara's, and to a lesser degree Jamie's, professional development during National Board candidacy.

Lustick and Sykes (2006) explain that the final 25% of NBPTS candidates experience *deferred learning*, which occurs when a candidate takes in information during completion of the NBPTS certification requirements but does not act on the information at that time. While candidates who fall into this category may alter their teaching practices to more closely align with the NBPTS standards at some later time, there is no guarantee that they will follow through beyond their certification year. Teachers who are uncertain as to whether or not learning took place during National Board candidacy may be deferred learners. Jamie's NBPTS certification experience most resembles Lustick and Sykes' (2006) description of deferred learning.

Clearly, considerable differences exist in the nature and degree of learning that occurred for Anne, Barbara, and Jamie through National Board candidacy. Chapter 7 explores the differences in learning experienced by the three teachers during their NBPTS certification year. Beginning with a comparison of their experiences and readiness for learning prior to National Board candidacy, the chapter explores several possible explanations for Jamie's tenuous learning experience.

Prior Experiences and Readiness for Learning

"Good teachers are always doing professional development, and I'm finding that most of the people who are going through National Boards are the ones who have been lifelong learners. They are willing to adapt their teaching and try new things, read, work with other teachers, and do what benefits students rather than what's most easy for the teacher."

~Barbara, January 2005

Although Anne, Barbara, and Jamie approached the NBPTS certification experience for different reasons and along different paths and timelines, the three teachers share much in common regarding their prior experiences and readiness for National Board candidacy. Five particular themes emerge most prominently.

Strong Foundation of Education and Teaching Experience

At the time that they embarked upon National Board candidacy, Anne, Barbara, and Jamie each had between 16 and 20 years of teaching experience. While Anne and Jamie had always taught fifth grade, Barbara had experience teaching kindergarten through fifth grade in addition to serving as a reading specialist for seven years. Also at the time they began the certification process, all three teachers held master's degrees, and Barbara, certified in Reading Recovery, had completed 48 semester hours of graduate coursework beyond her master's.

The fact that the three teachers were well educated and experienced by the time they decided to pursue National Board certification is consistent with findings from other studies. In an analysis of data from 251, 567 North Carolina teachers, one study found that NBPTS applicants are more likely to be female, to have earned their teaching license through traditional means, to hold a master's degree, and to score well on standardized tests (Goldhaber, Perry, &

Anthony, 2003). Similarly, in their study of 775 NBPTS math and science candidates, Pyke and Lynch (2005) found that the majority of their respondents were white, female, over 40, had more than ten years of teaching experience, and held a master's degree.

A third survey reported that 62.5% of 32 Indiana NBCTs had completed five to 15 years of teaching experience and 31% had earned a master's degree before beginning National Board candidacy (NBPTS, 2002); while yet another survey found that 88% of 35 Arizona NBCTs held a master's degree and 82% of those with a master's had taken additional graduate classes as well (Vandevoort et al., 2004). Similarly, in three related studies exploring readiness for National Board candidacy, all six teachers interviewed held master's degrees at the time they began the NBPTS certification experience, two having completed several semester hours of graduate coursework beyond the master's (Hunzicker, 2003a; Hunzicker, 2003b; Hunzicker, 2004). As Anne, Barbara, and Jamie confirm, a strong foundation of education and experience is common among teachers pursuing the challenge of National Board certification.

An Established Pattern of Lifelong Learning

In addition to ample education and teaching experience, Anne, Barbara, and Jamie demonstrate established patterns of ongoing professional growth. Throughout their careers, all three teachers have spent a great deal of time researching new ideas and trying new activities and approaches in their classrooms to keep their teaching fresh and current. Barbara and Jamie often seek new materials and methods to bolster their instruction, such as new works of children's literature and engaging learning activities. Anne is drawn to creative, open-ended projects through which her students can apply content-related skills and concepts.

In addition, all three teachers have developed their teaching effectiveness over the years through the trial-and-error process of accommodating student needs. Both Barbara and Jamie have been responsible for teaching classes that include subgroups of students with learning disabilities, and Jamie has taught classes that incorporate gifted and talented students. Additionally, both Barbara and Jamie have had to modify materials, instruction, and assessments for students with limited ability to communicate in English. Anne, who is responsible for delivering an accelerated curriculum to a class of students identified as gifted, also finds it necessary to accommodate a wide range of academic abilities each year. Moreover, Anne has learned a great deal about effective teaching through the trial-and-error process of managing student behavior within her classroom.

Of the three teachers, Anne is the least likely to leave her classroom for professional workshops and conferences, preferring instead to focus on her day to day work with students. Jamie enjoys attending professional development activities outside of her school as long as the topic is highly relevant to her classroom. Barbara, the most zealous of the three in regard to formal professional development, attends and presents at local, state, and national conferences on a regular basis. Barbara also participates regularly in study groups and other professional development opportunities offered within her school and district, sometimes assuming a leadership role during the process. In addition, professional reading is a key means of learning for Barbara. She has read widely and routinely throughout her teaching career.

At least two other studies document that teachers who pursue National Board certification frequently engage in ongoing professional development activities. In a survey of 32 Indiana NBCTs, 87.5% reported regularly attending professional workshops and 22% described NBPTS candidates as lifelong learners (NBPTS, 2002). In a second study, 97% of 35 Arizona NBCTs reported participating in professional growth activities on a regular basis (Vandevoort et al., 2004). When teachers remain highly motivated over time to expand their professional knowledge and skill, it makes sense that the pursuit of National Board certification serves as a natural extension of professional growth. Anne, Barbara, and Jamie are typical NBPTS candidates in this regard.

Independent Learners

Both Anne and Jamie share that they prefer to work independently, not only in their day to day teaching practice but also when engaging in challenging endeavors such as National Board certification. While Barbara works well alone, she also enjoys collaborating professionally with others, and does so often.

Although no research directly exploring the tendency of NBPTS candidates toward independent or collaborative learning exists at this time, studies suggest that teachers seeking National Board certification may be more independent than collaborative. In one study, principals rated NBCTs lower on relationships with colleagues than any other category (Vandevoort et al., 2004). In addition, several studies report increased collaboration with colleagues as a positive outcome of National Board candidacy (Anderson et al., 2001; Athanases, 1994; Chittenden & Jones, 1997; Kieffer-Barone et al., 1999; Mitchell, 1998; NBPTS, 2001b; Sato, 2000). These findings indicate that, although National Board candidates may become more collaborative as a result of the NBPTS certification process, they tend to be most comfortable learning independently. The experiences of Anne, Barbara, and Jamie support this idea.

Collaborative, Learner-Centered School Environments

Beyond a teacher's internal motivation to learn and grow professionally, working within a collaborative, learner-centered school environment provides further impetus toward lifelong learning and professional achievement. Throughout National Board candidacy, Anne, Barbara, and Jamie all spoke highly of their school environments and the colleagues with whom they worked. At least half of the certified staff in all three schools held master's degrees, with the highest percentage, 67%, at Anne's school. While no NBCTs were part of the faculty at Cady Stanton or CGS at the time that Barbara and Jamie began the certification process, Dickenson Gifted School boasted two NBCTs at the time that Anne embarked upon the endeavor.

Barbara cites numerous opportunities for professional development at Cady Stanton, identifying a recent initiative sponsored by the Ball Foundation, which involved collaborative research and the eventual school-wide implementation of reading and writing workshop, as one of the most significant learning experiences of her career. Anne, reflecting upon her achievement of National Board certification, acknowledges Dickenson's school environment as a key element of her success. She explains, "We teach there because we're creative people. We're expected to think outside of the box, to integrate community experiences, to communicate closely with families. I do those things every day, so it was easy to bring them into my portfolio entries. It's how we think at our school. I think that might be an advantage that teachers in a school like ours have over others in earning NBPTS certification."

Anne's analysis is consistent with the findings of one study, which concludes that teachers working within a collaborative school culture are more likely to successfully complete the NBPTS requirements due to the abundance of resources available (Hunzicker, 2003b). Similarly, a study by Goldhaber and colleagues (2003) found that teachers are more likely to apply for NBPTS certification if other teachers in their district are currently going through the process, and that teaching in a school with NBCTs during National Board candidacy increases a candidate's chances of earning the certification.

Conversely, teaching in a school with unsuccessful NBPTS candidates may negatively affect the likelihood of earning certification (Goldhaber et al., 2003). Two additional studies found that teachers in urban and suburban school districts with healthy budgets and positive student achievement trends find more support during National Board candidacy than do teachers in low performing schools (Linquanti & Peterson, 2001), rural schools, and high poverty schools (Rotberg, Futtrell, & Holmes, 2000).

Ripe for a New Professional Challenge

Perhaps most significantly, all three teachers were first interested in pursuing National Board certification because it offered a form of professional development that they had never before experienced. Anne was seeking a new professional challenge but did not want to leave Dickenson, and Jamie wanted to take more graduate courses but could not find classes in which she was interested. The NBPTS certification process provided a beneficial resolution for both of them. Barbara, who had considered seeking National Board certification years earlier but did not want to take the written assessment, also reached a point where she felt ready to accept a new and unfamiliar professional challenge.

The motivation of all three teachers is consistent with a survey of 519 California NBCTs in which 84% of respondents identified personal challenge as their primary reason for pursuing the certification. In the same study, 79% cited the certification as an opportunity for professional development to strengthen their teaching practices (CFTL, 2002). Similarly, 25% of 32 NBCTs from Indiana described teachers who seek NBPTS certification as individuals who enjoy challenge (NBPTS, 2002).

The Importance of Financial Support

Although they were initially drawn to the NBPTS certification process because it was a unique form of professional development, Anne, Barbara, and Jamie each viewed the annual stipends paid to NBCTs by their school districts and the State of Illinois as attractive incentives. Numerous studies identify money as a motivating factor for teachers considering the pursuit of National Board certification.

It has become common for teachers to receive financial support as an incentive for pursuing National Board certification. One hundred percent of 35 Arizona NBCTs in one study (Vandevoort et al., 2004) and 90% of 120 NBPTS science candidates in a second study (Lustick & Sykes, 2006) received some form of financial incentive or support before, during, and/or following National Board candidacy. Moreover, an analysis of data from 251, 567 North Carolina teachers revealed that NBPTS applicants were 50% more likely to teach in a district that offered at least one form of financial incentive (Goldhaber et al., 2003). Similarly, in a series of studies exploring teachers' reasons for seeking National Board candidacy, all of the six teachers interviewed reported that their decision was influenced by the fact that the state was willing to pay their $3, 000 NBPTS registration fees (Hunzicker, 2003a; Hunzicker, 2003b; Hunzicker, 2004).

Further, one study indicates that financial support and incentives for pursuing National Board certification may encourage candidates' and NBCTs' commitment to the teaching profession. In a survey of 32 Indiana NBCTs, 12.5% felt obligated to complete the certification process since the registration fee had been paid by their school district or state (NBPTS, 2002). Further, Lustick and Sykes (2006) conclude that, because mounting evidence shows that teachers are learning through the NBPTS certification experience, financial support and incentives encouraging teachers toward National Board certification are warranted.

Anne, Barbara, and Jamie each approached the NBPTS certification process with a strong foundation of education and teaching experience, each demonstrating an established pattern of lifelong learning. Describing themselves as primarily independent learners, all three teachers enjoyed working in collaborative, learner-centered school environments at the time of their National Board candidacy. In addition, all three teachers decided to pursue NBPTS certification because they were at a point in their teaching careers where they were ripe for a new professional challenge.

Overall, the prior experiences and readiness reported by Anne, Barbara, and Jamie are consistent with the findings of previous studies exploring teachers' paths toward NBPTS certification. However, while Anne and Barbara report numerous examples of learning as a result of the experience, Jamie does not. Further, Anne and Barbara were successful in earning National Board certification; Jamie was not.

Like Anne and Barbara, Jamie demonstrated numerous examples of accomplished teaching during her certification year, yet she struggled throughout the certification process.

For this reason, the conditions that may have affected her certification experience are worth exploring further. With this purpose in mind, the second half of Chapter 7 looks closely at possible reasons for Jamie's tenuous learning experience during National Board candidacy.

Conditions Working against Jamie

"National Board Certification isn't only about showcasing what you do well, it's also about facing what you don't do well, creating a self improvement plan and recognizing that you, the teacher, are a learner too."

~Moseley & Rains, 2002, p. 47

Although their prior experiences and readiness for learning were similar at the outset of National Board candidacy, key differences in the conditions surrounding the three teachers became apparent as they engaged in the certification process. One condition that may have affected Jamie's difficult learning experience was limited collaborative support.

Limited Collaborative Support

Anne, Barbara, and Jamie differed significantly in the amount of collaborative support they received during National Board candidacy. Throughout their NBPTS certification experiences, Anne and Barbara participated regularly in local support group meetings led by NBCTs. In addition, Anne was mentored closely by two NBCTs in her school, and Barbara received feedback and advice from two NBCTs in her school district. Moreover, Barbara frequently exchanged ideas and information with fellow candidates from across the nation in online chat rooms.

In contrast, Jamie was the only Middle Childhood Generalist candidate in her region during the 2004-2005 school year. Although she engaged in an independent study through a local university, attended support meetings offered by the Regional Office of Education, and consulted regularly with a friend and NBPTS candidate who was seeking certification in Literacy: Reading/Language Arts, she felt alone throughout most her NBPTS certification experience.

Numerous studies document the importance of providing support to NBPTS candidates (Athanases, 1994; Kanter et al., 2000; Keiffer-Barone et al., 1999; Linquanti & Peterson, 2001; Rotberg et al., 2000). In Vandevoort and colleagues' (2004) survey of 35 Arizona NBCTs, 81% received university-based support, 77% were given release time to work on the certification requirements, and 74% worked closely with a mentor. In a second study, 79.5% of 5, 641 NBPTS candidates surveyed reported participating in an organized support group during their certification year (NBPTS, 2001b).

Moreover, research shows that while both financial and moral support are important, collaboration with others who understand the National Board standards and requirements is essential. Exploring the certification year support of five National Board candidates in the Midwest, Keiffer-Barone and colleagues (1999) found that teachers benefit most from support groups led by NBCTs paired with ongoing collaboration and support from fellow candidates. Similarly, a survey of 92 NBCTs and National Board candidates in North Carolina identified opportunities to dialogue with peers and mentors as one of the most helpful attributes of the support groups (Anderson et al., 2001).

It makes sense that collaboration with knowledgeable others during National Board candidacy supports teacher learning and increases the likelihood of earning NBPTS certification. Throughout her certification experience, Jamie yearned for more collaboration so that she could "bounce ideas off" others. She also wished for opportunities to visit the classrooms of other teachers and host them in visiting hers. The fact that Jamie received significantly less collaborative support than both Anne and Barbara very likely contributed to the difficulties she experienced in completing the NBPTS certification requirements, and may have limited her learning during the experience as well.

However, the fact that many teachers working in isolation and/or with limited support are successful in achieving National Board certification (Hunzicker, 2003a;

Kanter et al. 2000; Pyke & Lynch, 2005) argues against the possibility that Jamie's difficult certification experience and lack of learning are due to limited collaborative support alone. In one survey of 32 Indiana NBCTs, 22% had minimal to no collaborative support during National Board candidacy, and 44% had no mentor support during the process (NBPTS, 2002). Additionally, a second study concludes that although more teachers seem to prefer a group-supported certification experience, the chances of earning National Board certification are no greater when requirements are completed with group support than when they are completed independently (Pyke & Lynch, 2005).

Jamie describes herself as a person who prefers to work alone and most values professional development that allows her to make improvements within her own classroom. However, even though the style of professional development offered by the NBPTS aligns closely with her stated learning preferences, she feels strongly that her certification experience was diminished due to lack of collaborative support. Backing Jamie's assertion, Pyke and Lynch (2005) state that the level of collaborative support during National Board candidacy is not the distinguishing factor in whether or not a teacher successfully earns NBPTS certification. Rather, a candidate's success is related to a close match between the individual and her preferred level of collaborative support.

Because Jamie's collaborative preferences and the collaborative support available to her during National Board candidacy were not well matched, it is likely that limited collaborative support was one condition affecting her tenuous certification experience. However, additional explanations are likely. Exploring further, Jamie's low level of alignment to the NBPTS standards at the outset of her certification experience is a second condition that may have contributed to her difficulties.

Low Alignment to the NBPTS Standards

An increasing number of studies recognize that teachers approach National Board candidacy at varying levels of accomplished teaching, which can affect the amount of

147

learning that occurs during the experience (Lustick, 2002; Lustick & Sykes, 2006; Pyke & Lynch, 2005). One study, which explored teacher learning outcomes by comparing the thought processes and performance of ten Michigan science teachers before and after the certification experience, describes four most readily observed National Board candidate types based in part on their alignment with the NBPTS standards at the outset of National Board candidacy (Lustick, 2002).

Type A candidates are teachers whose professional practice demonstrates a high degree of alignment with the NBPTS standards and expectations before ever beginning the certification process. During their certification experience, these teachers' professional practices are affirmed more than they are transformed. As a result, Type A candidates do not learn as much during the NBPTS certification experience but ultimately become National Board certified because they are able to authentically demonstrate accomplished teaching.

Type B candidates begin the NBPTS certification process without close alignment to the National Board standards but make significant changes to their teaching practices through the experience. Type B candidates undergo a great deal of learning through National Board candidacy and achieve NBPTS certification as a result. In Lustick's words, "These are the rare individuals who describe the process as 'life changing' and 'remarkable'" (2002, p. 9).

In distant alignment to the National Board standards at the outset of the certification experience, Type C candidates demonstrate willingness to try the ideas of the NBPTS, yet they are not able to align their teaching practices closely enough to the standards to achieve the certification. Even so, Type C candidates often learn a great deal during National Board candidacy. Lustick describes the Type C candidate as "potentially one of the most numerous of the identified types" (2002, p. 9).

Type D candidates are teachers whose professional practice was aligned only minimally to the National Board standards at the outset of the certification experience and remains relatively unchanged throughout the process. Lustick writes, "These teachers tended to hold on to their ideas, values, and beliefs about teaching and learning with an iron fist. They viewed their work as not complex and quite certain. For this type, teaching is like a science that is validated from their many years of experience. Isolation is not a problem, but a virtue of practice. They enjoy the autonomy and freedom isolation brings and express little desire to discuss pedagogical issues with colleagues or be involved in anything outside their immediate sphere of control. This type of candidate may express resentment, hostility, or suspicion regarding the National Board and the certification process. Though Type D candidates may be quite effective at bringing about learning in students, their approach, ideas, values, and beliefs may not be in agreement with those of the National Board" (2002, p. 9).

Classified according to Lustick's (2002) NBPTS candidate types, Barbara appears to be a Type A candidate, Anne aligns closely with the Type B description, and Jamie most closely fits the Type D disposition. As a Type D candidate, Jamie was not in close alignment with the National Board standards at the outset of her certification experience. Coupled with limited collaborative support, the conditions that may have adversely affected Jamie's learning through National Board candidacy begin to take shape. A third contributing explanation is her negative outlook.

Jamie's Negative Outlook

In addition to differing levels of collaborative support and varying levels of alignment to the NBPTS standards, Anne, Barbara, and Jamie each navigated the National Board certification experience with distinctive outlooks. When Barbara finally began the certification process, after years of pursuing other forms of professional development, she was the most confident of the three because she had built up a wealth of professional experiences from which to draw. She was motivated to pursue National Board certification because she believed that it would affirm her established teaching practices and give her more credibility as a professional. During the process, Barbara studied and adjusted to the NBPTS standards and requirements within the context of professional practices that she had customized through years of experience.

Of the three teachers, Anne appeared to be the most determined to complete the NBPTS certification requirements because it was her second attempt. Formally withdrawing during the 2003-2004 school year due to the illness and passing of her father, she relied heavily on the process the following year to guide her in meeting the needs of a very difficult class. Throughout the certification experience, Anne persistently reconsidered and started over when she discovered gaps between her teaching practice and the standards and requirements of the NBPTS. Trusting the values of the National Board implicitly, she readily made every effort to align with them.

Initially, Jamie approached her certification experience with a mixture of curiosity and willingness to try. Anticipating that completion of the certification requirements would be comparable to professional projects she had completed in the past, she resolved to take one step at a time and do the best that she could. But as she immersed herself in the process, disenchantment began to surface. She began questioning the descriptions of accomplished teaching in the NBPTS literature as well as the requirements for earning the certification. She also expressed reservations about the motives of the NBPTS and the government funding that supported it. As her doubt increased, Jamie became closed to adjusting her teaching practices to more closely align with the National Board.

Jamie's negative outlook toward the NBPTS certification process is a third condition that likely affected the nature and degree of her learning during National Board candidacy. Progressing from indifference to distrust over the course of her certification year, her outlook eventually hardened to resistance. Numerous studies have established trust as a requisite that must be in place before learning can occur (Glasser, 1997; Jensen, 1998; McCarty, 1993), but why was Jamie so distrustful? She was motivated to pursue NBPTS certification at the outset, and her prior experiences and readiness for learning were similar to Anne's, Barbara's, and most other teachers across the nation who have chosen to pursue the certification; yet she struggled significantly. Closer examination of the "symptoms" that emerged during Jamie's certification experience enables us to further understand her resistance to learning during National Board candidacy.

Understanding Jamie's Resistance

"Some highly articulate teachers may become certified and some less articulate teachers may miss out, and the fault may be in their ease or difficulty translating personal, practical, knowledge-in-action into a form of knowledge-about-action that is amenable to assessment in conventional ways."

~Vandevoort et al., 2004 p. 9

Beyond the conditions of limited collaborative support, low alignment to the NBPTS standards, and a negative outlook toward the certification process, two specific factors fueled Jamie's mounting resistance as she engaged in the certification experience: difficulty writing the NBPTS portfolio entries and unwillingness to adjust her teaching practices to more closely align with the NBPTS standards. Exploring Jamie's resistance through these specific factors helps to uncover the underlying reason for her tenuous certification experience: rejection of the NBPTS discourse.

Difficulty Representing Accomplished Teaching through Language

It makes sense that the act of teaching, day after day, requires very different skills than describing and analyzing teaching practice in writing. Even with the support of videotapes and samples of student work, representing one's teaching practice through the written word may or may not capture the essence of a teacher's true performance. In addition to writing skills, NBPTS candidates must be able to analyze their teaching practice beyond observable behavior. In order to provide the research-based rationale for their instructional decisions, required for successful NBPTS

151

portfolio completion, teachers must be able to articulate their tacit knowledge (Burroughs, 2001; Sato, 2000; Vandevoort et al., 2004) and recognize that the teaching/learning process is influenced by a multitude of extraneous variables (Chittenden & Jones, 1997; Danielson, 1996; Lustick, 2002).

More than one study cautions that teachers who have difficulty articulating their teaching practices within the NBPTS requirements may not be able to successfully demonstrate accomplished teaching through the NBPTS portfolio (Burroughs, Schwartz, & Hendricks-Lee, 2000; Burroughs, 2001; Lustick & Sykes, 2006; Sato, 2000: Vandevoort et al., 2004). In fact, one researcher asserts that rhetorical skill, the ability to write to an unknown audience in an unfamiliar genre from an outside position, is an unarticulated standard of the NBPTS (Burroughs, 2001). Conversely, evidence exists that some teachers may be able to earn National Board certification without truly being accomplished teachers (Pool, Ellet, Schiavone, & Carey-Lewis, 2001). Studies such as these suggest that the National Board's system for identifying master teachers may not be foolproof.

Throughout Jamie's certification experience, numerous examples of accomplished teaching practice, as described by the NBPTS, could be observed in her classroom. However, even though NBCT mentors read her portfolio drafts and asked questions to help her view her teaching practice more deeply, working through the abstract medium of language was difficult for Jamie. Both talking and writing about her teaching were more challenging for her than the act of teaching itself. It is possible that Jamie's difficulty completing requirements for the NBPTS portfolio was not because her teaching practice failed to meet the expectations of the National Board. It may have more to do with her inability to articulate and analyze her teaching practice through the medium of written language.

If this is the case, collaborative support could have made a difference for Jamie, both in earning National Board certification and in learning through the experience. Fellow NBPTS candidates observing in her classroom may have been able to point out examples of accomplished teaching practice that she might not have recognized otherwise. NBCT mentors may have been able to identify aspects of her teaching that she could most easily adjust in order to more closely align with the standards of the National Board.

With or without collaborative support, Jamie's inability to adequately represent her teaching practice through the medium of written language was a key factor in her mounting frustration and distrust of the NBPTS certification process. However, this still does not fully explain the lack of learning that occurred for her during National Board candidacy. Strategic decisions that she made throughout her certification experience were an important factor as well, especially in regard to showcasing "as is" teaching practices in her NBPTS portfolio.

Showcasing "As Is" Teaching Practices

Chittenden and Jones (1997) noted the tension experienced by ten New Jersey teachers during NBPTS portfolio completion as they balanced showcasing actual samples of their teaching with pleasing the NBPTS assessors. The teachers in their study reported struggling to maintain their authenticity while simultaneously integrating the standards and addressing the questions required for each portfolio entry. As a result of their struggle, not all teachers in the study were able to achieve a satisfactory balance between their individuality and the NBPTS portfolio requirements, and not all were successful in earning National Board certification.

Similarly, Gaddis's (2002) study of four National Board candidates' decision-making during completion of the portfolio describes teachers' in-progress feelings and reasoning. In her study, teachers based decisions about what to include in their portfolios on their beliefs about what was best for students paired with what was most likely to result in National Board certification. Comparing their teaching practices to the NBPTS standards, candidates experienced feelings of disequilibrium when they discovered discrepancies between the two. In an attempt to resolve their feelings of disequilibrium, the teachers further scrutinized their teaching practice to find evidence of alignment that they may have overlooked the first time, or they altered their teaching practices in order to include evidence of the standards.

In both studies, teachers experienced discomfort during completion of the NBPTS portfolio when showcasing their "as is" teaching practices fell short of National Board expectations. In addition, some teachers made an effort to adjust their teaching practices to more closely align with the NBPTS standards and requirements for portfolio completion while others did not.

Both Anne and Barbara experienced disequilibrium during completion of the NBPTS portfolio, and both proactively adjusted their teaching practice to align with National Board expectations. When Anne's students were in the midst of creating electrified haunted houses to culminate a science unit on electricity, she realized that the project did not directly and completely address the unit's instructional goals. As a result, she did not use the electricity unit for her NBPTS portfolio as originally intended but instead planned a science unit on sound that was more likely to meet the expectations of the National Board.

Even Barbara, who was teaching in close alignment to the NBPTS standards prior to her certification experience, made adjustments to her teaching practice in order to earn the highest scores possible on her NBPTS portfolio. Teaching two genres of writing within four weeks' time and assigning content-related writing topics instead of allowing students to select their own topics was probably the most significant instructional adjustment that Barbara made during National Board candidacy. While she was extremely uncomfortable at the time, she realized through the experience that there are effective means of teaching writing in addition to her own methods.

Finding a balance between showcasing "as is" teaching practices and adjusting teaching to more closely align with NBPTS expectations is perhaps the greatest challenge of National Board candidacy. Most teachers who pursue the certification must alter their teaching practices in order to successfully complete the requirements. Jamie was not willing to make adjustments to her teaching practice in order to more closely align with National Board expectations. She felt strongly that to do so would create a fraudulent representation of her teaching practice.

While she sometimes altered her routine, such as integrating math, science, and technology into one lesson for Portfolio Entry 3; she did not fundamentally change her teaching practice in order to increase her chances of earning NBPTS certification. By limiting her certification experience to showcasing "as is" teaching, Jamie demonstrated her rejection of the National Board discourse. Whether she did this consciously or subconsciously, her steadfast rejection most fully explains the difficulty she experienced throughout the certification process, as well as the most likely reason for her limited learning during the experience.

Rejecting the NBPTS Discourse

Recognizing that some National Board candidates have trouble representing their teaching practice through the medium of written language, Burroughs and colleagues (2000) explain that the NBPTS certification process can be classified as a written discourse community. They define the term as "a social entity within which a set of distinctive writing practices occur and beyond whose borders different writing practices occur" (Beaufort, 1997 as cited in Burroughs et al., 2000, pp. 345-346).

In order to successfully navigate the discourse of the NBPTS, a teacher must first apply the hypothetical descriptions of accomplished teaching from the NBPTS literature to the context of a "real" classroom. Next, the teacher must select poignant samples of teaching and learning from actual classroom experiences to represent overall teaching performance. Finally, the teacher must articulate these samples using written language. Burroughs and colleagues assert that because the NBPTS certification process is a written discourse community "candidates are certified based on their language about their teaching, not their teaching itself" (2000, p. 349).

Navigating the NBPTS discourse is incredibly demanding. Not only must National Board candidates be convinced that they can successfully showcase their teaching practice through written language, they must also believe that they can accurately and convincingly represent their teaching through samples, such as a brief, unedited videotape or students' graded assignments. Moreover, candidates must be willing to move closer to the values, knowledge, language, and practices endorsed by the NBPTS, especially when the NBPTS discourse does not align closely with their own beliefs and teaching practices. If a candidate does not "buy in" to the discourse of the National Board, she will experience great difficulty throughout the process, and her chances of earning the certification will be diminished.

On occasion, both Anne and Barbara objected to the challenges of completing the NBPTS portfolio, yet both tenaciously made adjustments to their teaching practices and portfolio entries to increase their chances of earning the certification. Through their persistence and willingness to adjust, they demonstrated acceptance of the NBPTS discourse and its values, learned as a result of the experience, and were rewarded with National Board certification.

Conversely, Jamie chose not to make adjustments to her teaching practice in order to become National Board certified, which limited her learning during National Board candidacy more than any other factor. By rejecting the standards, expectations, and requirements of the NBPTS, Jamie forfeited her opportunity to earn National Board certification.

Is Jamie's NBPTS Learning Experience Atypical?

Jamie's tenuous certification experience was due to a combination of adverse conditions and internal resistance. Limited collaborative support, low alignment to the NBPTS standards, and a negative outlook contributed to her frustration toward the written discourse community of the NBPTS. While her resistance mounted as she struggled to represent her teaching practice through the medium of written language, her inflexibility in showcasing "as is" teaching practices at the expense of striving toward closer alignment to the National Board standards worked against her more than any other factor. Unfortunately, Jamie's unwillingness to accept the standards, values, and requirements that make up the NBPTS discourse significantly limited her learning during National Board candidacy and ultimately prevented her from achieving NBPTS certification.

Roughly one third of National Board candidates nationwide achieve NBPTS certification on their first attempt. During the year that Anne, Barbara, and Jamie pursued the certification, 36% of all first-time candidates were successful (Sandy-Hanson, personal communication, February 10, 2006). While teachers who do not accomplish the NBPTS requirements on their first try can re-attempt the sections they failed for up to two years, many do not have the wherewithal to try again. Others persist, and some are eventually rewarded with NBCT status.

In regard to the overall achievement rate of NBPTS certification, Jamie's experience is not atypical. During the 2004-2005 school year, she was one of the 64% of National Board candidates who did not pass the requirements. However, her limited learning during National Board candidacy is much less common. The overwhelming majority of teachers who have experienced the NBPTS certification process describe it as an outstanding form of professional development (Bohen, 2001; CFTL, 2002; Kanter et al., 2000; Keiffer-Barone, et al., 1999; Linquanti & Peterson, 2001; Moseley & Rains, 2003; NBPTS, 2001a; Rotberg et al., 2000; & Thornton, 2001), and one of the first scientific studies to examine teacher learning during National Board candidacy concludes that the majority of teachers do indeed learn as a result of the experience (Lustick & Sykes, 2006). Jamie is one of very few who report learning little through the process.

One documented NBPTS certification experience that closely mirrors Jamie's is that of Joy, an African-American kindergarten teacher working in an urban, low income school setting (Burroughs et al., 2000; Burroughs, 2001). Although Joy began her certification year generally accepting the NBPTS standards and requirements, she became frustrated with the process as she worked to complete the portfolio entries, eventually concluding that she was incapable of capturing the essence of her teaching practice through writing and that the NBPTS could not accurately evaluate her teaching practice without multiple on-site observations. Although she rejected the NBPTS discourse, Joy persisted in completing the certification requirements. However, she did not earn National Board certification.

Certification experiences such as Joy's and Jamie's appear to be uncommon although at least three studies acknowledge that not all teachers experience a great deal of learning as a result of National Board candidacy. In one study, the majority of teachers felt that their professional practice had improved through the NBPTS certification process, yet some reported that their teaching did not change as a result of the experience (Tracz et al., 1995). In a second study, one of 28 NBCTs participating in a focus group discussion disagreed with the statement that the process of NBPTS certification had made him a more effective teacher (NBPTS, 2002). Further, Lustick and Sykes (2006) estimate that 25% of NBPTS candidates experience deferred learning during National Board candidacy and may or may not alter their teaching practices to more closely align with the National Board standards at some later time.

So, although other NBPTS candidates' difficult learning experiences remain largely undocumented at this time, it stands to reason that *Jamie's certification experience is more representative than it is unusual.* Clearly, more research is needed to tell the stories of teachers such as Jamie and Joy so that we can better understand – and overcome – barriers to teacher learning during National Board candidacy.

8

The Leverage of National Board Candidacy

Anne, Barbara, and Jamie provide us with an inside view of National Board candidacy. Observing their teaching practices, guiding philosophies, and thought processes, we get to know them as teachers. Hearing their reflections about the certification experience and their personal accounts of learning, we are able to identify both general outcomes of teacher learning and factors that may support or hinder learning during the certification process. Comparing their experiences to those of others who have completed NBPTS certification requirements further develops our understanding of teacher learning during the certification year.

The customized nature of teacher learning through National Board candidacy is illustrated vividly through the differences in the certification experiences of the three teachers. Beyond Anne's enthusiastic determination, Barbara's confident presentation, and Jamie's tentative curiosity, an infinite range of NBPTS certification experiences abound. While the identification of National Board candidate types such as those identified by Lustick (2002) provide an important starting point for understanding teacher learning through National Board candidacy, the dynamic complexity of the experience also must be considered.

Following a brief overview of research identifying characteristics of the NBPTS certification process that promote teacher learning, Chapter 8 presents the idea of leverage during National Board candidacy. Consisting of three, ever-changing dynamics affected by teacher interaction with the NBPTS discourse, it is the leverage of National Board candidacy that either enhances or discourages teacher learning.

Promoting Teacher Learning through NBPTS Candidacy

"Teacher learning appears to occur through task structures that require teachers to learn new content and teaching strategies as part of their demonstration of performance and through the processes of required reflection."

~Darling-Hammond, 2001, p. 1

The substantial leverage of NBPTS certification is an impetus toward teacher learning that should not go unnoticed. Just as the simple machine called a lever can be used to force physical motion, the National Board certification process can strongly influence – or force – teaching beliefs and behaviors in a way that typical professional development experiences do not.

Simply reading or hearing about an idea is usually not enough to cause a teacher to make a significant change, especially if an established method of instruction is perceived by the teacher as "working." But the portfolio requirements of the NBPTS are rigorous and very specific, and because there are often gaps between the National Board standards and candidates' teaching practices, teachers have no choice but to modify their teaching to fit the requirements of the NBPTS to ensure a passing score. Barbara's resistance to abiding by NBPTS requirements in regard to student writing is one example. Had she not been forced to approach writing instruction differently to successfully complete one of her portfolio entries, she probably never would have become convinced that students can respond to teacher-driven topics, nor would she have realized that students can master different genres of writing within a shorter time period than she typically allotted.

At least one other study begins to articulate the idea of leverage as a key aspect of teacher learning through National Board candidacy. In this study, 17 California teachers who completed the NBPTS certification requirements during the 1998-1999 school year admitted that construction of the NBPTS portfolio prompted them to try teaching methods *that they would not otherwise have tried* and that preparing for the written assessment challenged them to review and engage in subject area content *that they would not otherwise have considered* (Sato, 2000).

Further, researchers are beginning to clarify characteristics of the NBPTS certification process that make it such a powerful professional development experience. Sato (2000) writes that the process contributes to teacher learning by providing a framework for self-evaluation, a benchmark for accomplished teaching, and a structure for examining teaching practice through evidence and artifacts. Keiffer-Barone and colleagues (1999) credit the combination of structure, through the NBPTS standards, and pressure, through the task of portfolio completion, in sustaining high levels of teacher learning throughout the process.

Moreover, Chittenden and Jones (1997) identify five characteristics of the NBPTS certification experience that promote teacher learning: 1.) It establishes a framework that includes a vision of effective teaching and a system for critical analysis, 2.) It provides a process for connecting the abstraction of standards to the reality of the classroom, 3.) It calls for systematic collaboration with other teachers, 4.) It demands persistence amidst the ongoing pressures of teaching, and 5.) It requires a high degree of accountability through formative and summative evaluation against a rigorous set of teaching standards.

All three studies identify high standards around a structured process of self-evaluation as elements of the NBPTS certification process that promote teacher learning. Additionally, two of the three recognize that the pressure of the experience somehow encourages teacher learning.

Chittenden and Jones (1997) further identify collaboration, accountability, and rigor as key components of the learning experience. The findings of these studies are helpful in articulating the characteristics and conditions that make the NBPTS certification process such a powerful form of professional development.

But beyond the static characteristics and conditions, National Board candidacy is dynamic since its structures and processes are dependent upon teacher interaction with the NBPTS discourse. As candidates read the descriptions of accomplished teaching presented in the NBPTS literature, apply research-based teaching practices within their own classrooms, select samples of their practice to represent overall teaching performance, and engage in the process of constant reflection and analysis, they are interacting with the discourse of the National Board. It is this interaction that customizes teacher learning as it occurs through the NBPTS certification experience. Through this interaction, the leverage of National Board candidacy is created.

The Leverage of National Board Candidacy

Within the context of National Board candidacy, *leverage* can be defined as an interactive dynamic between an individual and highly motivating conditions that demands teacher learning. Because of the leverage of National Board candidacy, it is difficult for a teacher *not* to learn through the experience. However, while the outcome of leverage is predominantly positive, the process is not always comfortable. In fact, most NBPTS candidates describe their certification experience as extremely challenging (Burroughs et al., 2000; CFTL, 2002; Linquanti & Peterson, 2001; Moseley & Rains, 2003; Rotberg et al., 2000, & Thornton, 2001) and highly stressful (Hunzicker, 2003a; Hunzicker, 2003b; Hunzicker, 2004). The leverage of National Board candidacy, then, is an interactive dynamic of positive pressure that, while uncomfortable, usually leads to substantial teacher learning.

The leverage of National Board candidacy consists of three dynamics: rigor, reward, and risk. The first dynamic, *rigor*, embodies the high expectations of the NBPTS. In order to achieve National Board certification, teachers must demonstrate accomplished teaching practice as described in the NBPTS literature. Using research-based methods, candidates must exhibit intentional teaching and respect for students as individuals in addition to presenting evidence of student progress over time. Only the highest professional standards are acceptable.

Reward, the second dynamic of leverage, encompasses the prestige of National Board certification. Because the certification is very difficult to achieve, becoming an NBCT is a significant accomplishment. In addition to increased status, respect, and professional authority, many NBCTs receive salary increases and/or state stipends as well. These "carrots" are highly motivating to many teachers who choose to pursue National Board certification.

The third dynamic, *risk*, accounts for the fact that two out of three NBPTS candidates fail to earn the certification on their first attempt. Seeking National Board certification involves huge professional risk because it is both public and confrontational. Unlike earning a master's degree, which can be accomplished quietly and even sporadically over time, National Board candidates complete the certification process within a specified timeframe, are forced to confront their professional weaknesses, and receive their yes-or-no certification results on the same well-publicized date nationwide. Because of the professional risk involved, many teachers never attempt the process while those who do usually feel anxious throughout the experience.

Working together, the dynamics of rigor, reward, and risk create the positive but uncomfortable pressure known well by teachers who have experienced the NBPTS certification process. To visualize the leverage of National Board candidacy, picture a triangle. Made up of three sides, the triangle itself represents leverage while its three sides represent rigor, reward, and risk (see Figure A).

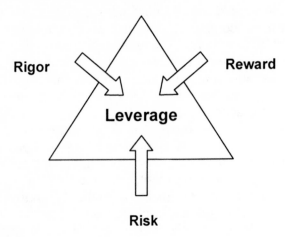

Figure A
The Leverage of National Board Candidacy

In concert with the three dynamics that create the leverage of National Board candidacy, teachers' motivational responses to each dynamic further reinforce the pressure experienced during the certification process (see Figure B). Candidates who respond strongly to the dynamic of rigor are those most interested in learning through National Board candidacy. They are invigorated by challenge and determined to improve their teaching. Teachers motivated by the dynamic of reward are most interested in the prestige of National Board certification. Confident in their ability to demonstrate accomplished teaching, these candidates seek professional recognition and affirmation. Teachers most concerned with the dynamic of risk are motivated by fear. Worried that they may not be successful in completing the NBPTS certification requirements, these teachers either become passive in their doubt and skepticism or they redouble their efforts toward certification to avoid the embarrassment of failure.

Just as a triangle must have three sides, all three dynamics must be present to create leverage during National Board candidacy. Without all three, leverage during the process would not exist. However, while the dynamics of rigor, reward, and risk are part of every teacher's NBPTS certification experience, the degree of each dynamic varies from individual to individual. *The differences depend on each individual's motivations and/or responses to the certification process.*

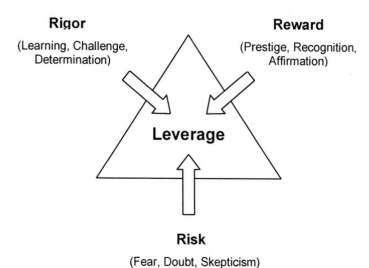

Rigor
(Learning, Challenge, Determination)

Reward
(Prestige, Recognition, Affirmation)

Leverage

Risk
(Fear, Doubt, Skepticism)

Figure B
The Leverage of National Board Candidacy with Teacher Motives/Responses Shown

Consider Anne, for example. Utterly determined to achieve NBPTS certification, she persisted in re-adjusting her teaching practice throughout her certification experience to more closely align with the standards and expectations of the National Board (see Figure C). The longest side of Anne's triangle is rigor because it was this dynamic that most motivated her during National Board candidacy. But, keep in mind that all three dynamics work together to create leverage. In addition, the three angles of a triangle can only add up to 180 degrees. So, if one dynamic is more influential than the others, the three sides of the triangle will vary in length.

In Anne's certification experience, the dynamic of reward was second most influential. Highly valuing the prestige that comes with being National Board certified, she constantly looked ahead to the reward that awaited her as she worked and learned throughout the certification process. While her awareness of professional risk was certainly a stressor during the experience, risk was the least influential of the three dynamics that created leverage for Anne during National Board candidacy. For Anne, the dynamic of risk motivated her to sustain her efforts, even during periods of self-doubt.

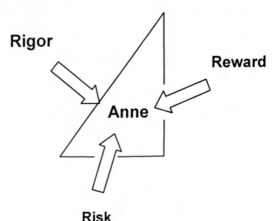

Figure C
Anne's Leverage during National Board Candidacy

While the three dynamics that create the leverage of National Board candidacy remain the same, Barbara's triangle looks different than Anne's (see Figure D). Above all else, Barbara sought affirmation of her teaching practices through NBPTS certification. While she was interested in learning through the experience, it was her desire to be National Board certified that motivated her most. With the dynamic of reward creating the longest side of Barbara's triangle and rigor close behind, the dynamic of risk played the smallest role in Barbara's certification experience. Like Anne, the idea of not achieving the certification motivated Barbara to do everything within her power to successfully complete the certification requirements. However, because of her confidence in her teaching ability, her fear was not as pronounced as Anne's.

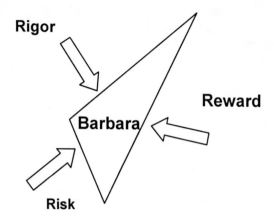

Figure D
Barbara's Leverage during National Board Candidacy

As might be expected, Jamie's triangle is shaped differently than either Anne's or Barbara's since the leverage that she experienced during National Board candidacy was different still (see Figure E). Risk dominated Jamie's certification experience, and as a result claims the longest side of her triangle. Although she welcomed the reward of National Board certification and expressed willingness early in the process to learn from the experience, her doubt and skepticism quickly overshadowed the constructive aspects of her candidacy. Jamie's growing distrust and eventual rejection of the NBPTS discourse prevented the positive pressures of leverage from prevailing. With reward as the second most influential dynamic of her certification experience and rigor the least dominant of the three, learning was not a priority for Jamie during National Board candidacy.

Throughout their certification experiences, Anne, Barbara, and Jamie responded differently to the three dynamics that create the leverage of National Board candidacy. Anne was motivated primarily by rigor, then reward, and finally risk. Barbara responded to reward first, rigor second, and risk last. Jamie viewed risk as most significant, followed by reward, and ending with rigor. All three teachers experienced the leverage of National Board candidacy, yet each teacher's experience was customized through varying interaction with the three dynamics.

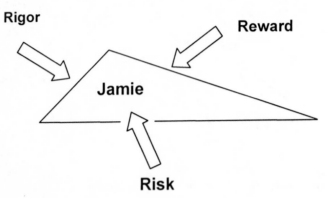

Figure E
Jamie's Leverage during National Board Candidacy

Corresponding Research

Interestingly, the varying dynamics of leverage experienced by the three teachers during National Board candidacy aligns closely with Lustick's (2002) NBPTS candidate types, described more thoroughly in Chapter 7. Anne, a Type B candidate, was not closely aligned with the NBPTS standards at the outset of her certification experience, but learned considerably during the process and ultimately achieved National Board certification. The significant learning experienced by Type B candidates parallels the dynamic of rigor, the longest side of Anne's triangle and the dynamic that motivated her most during National Board candidacy.

As a Type A candidate, Barbara was already teaching according to the expectations of the NBPTS at the time that she began the certification process. She did not learn a great deal during the experience but earned National Board certification by showcasing her established teaching practices. Correspondingly, Barbara's strongest dynamic during National Board candidacy was reward, with risk exerting the least amount of influence. Because Type A candidates are already accomplished teachers, the dynamics of rigor and risk are usually less influential than the dynamic of reward.

Jamie, a Type D candidate, was not demonstrating close alignment to the NBPTS standards when she began her certification experience, did not learn much during the process, and was not successful in achieving National Board certification. She so distrusted the NBPTS discourse that she could not avail herself to the act of learning through the experience. Correspondingly, the longest side of a Type D candidate's triangle is likely to be risk, and rigor the shortest. The fact that the varying dynamics for each of the three teachers parallels Lustick's (2002) NBPTS candidate types adds strength to the idea that some combination of rigor, reward, and risk creates leverage during National Board candidacy that usually results in teacher learning.

Further, Lustick and Sykes' (2006) NBPTS candidate learning types, summarized in Chapter 7, also relate to the three dynamics of leverage. Their description of dynamic learning (meaningful, immediate changes in teaching practice) aligns with the dynamic of rigor while technical learning (utilizing new teaching strategies in order to earn NBPTS certification) parallels the dynamic of reward. While these researchers' description of deferred learning (new information about teaching practice may be acted upon later) has the potential to align with the dynamic of rigor, it may also align with the dynamic of risk depending upon teacher action taken – or not – during and following the NBPTS certification experience. The important point of emphasis is that, to a large extent, the nature and degree of learning that occurs during National Board candidacy is within a teacher's control.

How Much Risk is "Too Much"?

While the "ideal" combination of rigor, reward, and risk is specific to each individual, we learn from Jamie's tenuous certification experience that too much emphasis on the dynamic of risk works against teachers regarding the amount of learning likely to occur during National Board candidacy as well as their chances of achieving NBPTS certification. But how much risk is "too much"? *Any time the dynamic of risk is greater than either the dynamic of rigor or the dynamic of reward, a teacher jeopardizes her chances of earning National Board certification.* Additionally, her potential for learning through the experience is compromised.

The leverage of National Board candidacy is an interactive dynamic between an individual and highly motivating conditions that demands teacher learning during the NBPTS certification experience. Consisting of rigor, reward, and risk, it creates an uncomfortable yet positive pressure that makes the pursuit of NBPTS certification one of the most powerful professional development experiences currently available to teachers.

We learn through the experiences of Anne, Barbara, and Jamie that the leverage of National Board candidacy can either propel teachers toward substantial learning and successful completion of the NBPTS certification requirements or create a downward spiral that discourages professional growth. With an understanding of the three dynamics that create leverage during National Board candidacy, teachers can approach the process better prepared for a successful certification experience.

Reading Group Guide

Part One: Establishing the Context

Chapter 1: Approaching National Board Candidacy

1.) Years before making the decision to seek National Board certification, Anne, Barbara, and Jamie each purposefully transferred to schools they believed were collaborative, learner-centered, and guided by educational research. What does this tell us about teachers who eventually pursue NBPTS certification? How important is a school's culture in supporting NBPTS candidates during their certification year? Explain. What elements or characteristics of school culture, if any, are most critical to the success of National Board candidates? Why do you think so?

Chapters 2 – 4: Anne, Barbara, and Jamie

2.) Of the three NBPTS candidates, Anne is the only one who was exposed to the NBPTS certification requirements prior to the year that she actually completed the process. Do you think this placed her at an advantage during her certification year? Why or why not? What other advantages did each of the three teachers bring to the certification experience? In your opinion, which are most important when considering a candidate's likelihood of earning National Board certification? Explain.

3.) Barbara shares that her professional development through the Ball Foundation influenced her teaching practice even more so than National Board candidacy. What does this tell us about Barbara as a learner? What does it tell us about her as a teacher? In what ways is Barbara's Ball

Foundation experience similar to National Board candidacy? How are the two different? What other examples of professional development might a teacher consider to be more powerful than the NBPTS certification experience? How might this information influence a teacher's decision to seek – or not to seek – National Board certification?

4.) All three teachers describe themselves as independent. In terms of successfully completing the requirements for NBPTS certification, do you think there could be an "ideal" balance between independence and collaboration? Does the "ideal" change when considering the two extremes in terms of day to day teaching? Why or why not? From a professional standpoint, where do you fall along this continuum? Should you choose to pursue NBPTS certification, how might this help or hinder your experience? Explain.

5.) At the beginning of Chapters 2, 3, and 4, the author uses three adjectives to describe each of the three teachers:
    Anne: Creative, Caring, Respectful
    Barbara: Confident, Student-centered, Firm
    Jamie: Committed, Rigorous, Fun
After reading the vignettes of the teaching practices, guiding philosophies, and thought processes of Anne, Barbara, and Jamie, do you think these adjectives accurately summarize each of the three teachers? Why or why not? Can you think of additional words that capture the essence of Anne, Barbara, and Jamie? Make a list for each teacher.

6.) In reading the descriptions of Anne, Barbara, and Jamie in Chapters 2, 3, and 4, several examples of accomplished teaching are described. For example, all three teachers prioritize students' needs and interests when planning instruction and related activities. What other examples of accomplished teaching stand out in the descriptions? Which do you find most impressive? Why? How does each teacher customize her teaching to actualize her own unique style? What have you learned about accomplished teaching from

Anne, Barbara, and/or Jamie after reading the vignettes describing their teaching practices?

7.) While the first three subheadings organizing the vignettes in Chapters 2, 3, and 4 are the same in each chapter, the fourth subheading is unique to each teacher:

Anne: Persisting toward Professional Growth

Barbara: Professional Leadership and Lifelong Learning

Jamie: Commitment to Students and their Achievement

How do these subject headings, and the accompanying vignettes, speak to the differences between the three teachers? In what ways might these differences influence each teacher's NBPTS certification experience? In what other ways are the three teachers different?

8.) Which of the three teachers is most like you? If you were a fourth or fifth grade student, in which class would you most like to be enrolled? What strengths and weaknesses can you identify in each teacher's style? In regard to areas of weakness, what suggestions might you offer? If Anne, Barbara, and Jamie were able to consider your suggestions, how do you think each teacher might respond?

Chapter 5: Reflecting on the NBPTS Certification Experience

9.) In Chapter 5, Anne describes National Board candidacy as "a big gamble" and Barbara calls it "a risky proposition". Do you agree with their assessments of the process? Why or why not? How is seeking NBPTS certification similar to and different from earning a graduate degree? Do you see one as being more valuable than the other? Explain.

10.) Both Anne and Jamie struggled with behaviorally challenging classes during the 2004-2005 school year. Anne feels strongly that the NBPTS ignores reality by not considering student behavior as a key aspect of the teaching context. While accomplished teaching in regard to classroom management is mentioned in the NBPTS literature, student behavior and motivation is not an emphasis of portfolio completion for Middle Childhood

Generalist certification. Barbara believes this is because teachers should not waste time focusing on their problems but should instead use their knowledge and skills to solve their problems. Which view do you believe is most accepted? How might knowledge of this issue help potential National Board candidates in preparation for, and during, their certification year?

11.) While NBPTS certification requires the completion of both a portfolio and a timed, written assessment, all three teachers place greater emphasis on the NBPTS portfolio when recalling their certification experiences. Why do you think the portfolio completion is the more significant aspect of the certification process for teachers? In what ways do you think completion of the portfolio contributes to, or detracts from, teacher learning during National Board candidacy? In what ways do you think it contributes to, or detracts from, the teaching and learning taking place within the classroom during the certification year? Can you think of a better way to configure the requirements for National Board certification? If so, describe your ideas.

12.) All three teachers supervised a student teacher during the 2004-2005 school year; Jamie during the fall semester, Anne during the spring semester, and Barbara during both semesters. While Barbara reports that having a student teacher supported her certification efforts, Jamie is neutral on the topic, and Anne strongly recommends that National Board candidates not accept student teachers during their certification year. Why do you think the three teachers experienced such diverse outcomes in regard to hosting student teachers during NBPTS candidacy? Do you agree with one teacher's viewpoint more than the others? Why or why not? What factors or conditions should potential candidates consider when making the decision to accept a student teacher – or not – during their certification year?

13.) Anne, Barbara, and Jamie each expressed frustration with the vague directions for portfolio completion provided in the NBPTS literature. Additionally, all three teachers were frustrated by the lack of specific feedback and guidance that they received through their NBCT-led support groups. Why do you think the "secret" of NBPTS portfolio completion is so well kept? Do you think the "mystery" of NBPTS portfolio completion supports or discourages teacher learning? If the NBPTS were to clarify their directions, or if NBCT-led support groups were to openly share examples of passing portfolio entries, how might the process and outcome of National Board certification be changed?

Part Two: Exploring Teacher Learning

Chapter 6: Teacher Learning through NBPTS Candidacy

14.) The style of professional development offered by the NBPTS combines application of research-based teaching practices with self-reflection and analysis of professional practice within a teacher's own classroom setting. Although this style aligns closely with Jamie's self-reported preference for professional growth, she shares that she did not learn as much as she expected during National Board candidacy. Do you think the process and requirements of NBPTS certification are optimally conducive to teacher learning? If so, what key characteristics do you believe make it a powerful vehicle of professional development? If not, what changes in the process and/or certification requirements might improve candidates' likelihood of learning through the experience?

15.) Reflecting on completion of the NBPTS portfolio, Barbara remarks, "I was learning all along, but not in the way that I typically recognize professional development. It wasn't until I started studying for the written assessment that it began feeling like professional development to me" (p. 114). Why do you think Barbara did not recognize that she was learning? What are the advantages of being unaware that learning is taking place? What are the disadvantages? How might a teacher expand her definition of professional development after completing a process such as NBPTS certification?

16.) Due to responsibility for gifted, learning disabled, Limited English Proficiency (LEP), and behaviorally challenged students over the years, all three teachers developed teaching effectiveness through the trial-and-error process of accommodating student needs prior to embarking upon National Board candidacy. How is this "natural" form of professional development similar to completion of the NBPTS portfolio? How might potential NBPTS candidates gain meaningful experiences with student subgroups before seeking National Board candidacy?

17.) During her certification experience, Jamie reports increased awareness of various aspects of effective teaching more than any other type of learning. How does awareness relate to readiness for learning? Which occurs first? Explain. How can NBPTS candidates use this information to optimize their learning during National Board candidacy?

18.) In synthesizing the learning of Anne, Barbara, and Jamie in Chapter 6, the author writes, "For at least some teachers who experience National Board candidacy, it appears that the whole of effective teaching does not extend far beyond the classroom" (p. 124). Where does "the whole" of effective teaching begin and end? How important is it for a teacher to understand "the whole" of effective teaching? Why? Within the "whole", which specific aspects of teaching should be a teacher's primary focus? What signs become apparent when a teacher begins to lose focus?

Chapter 7: Jamie's Tenuous Learning Experience
19.) Anne, Barbara, and Jamie each approached the NBPTS certification process with a strong foundation of education and teaching experience, as lifelong, primarily independent learners, as part of collaborative, learner-centered school environments, and ripe for a new professional challenge. Overall, the prior experiences and readiness reported by the three teachers are consistent with other studies exploring teachers' paths toward NBPTS

certification. Which of the five characteristics and conditions do you believe are most important in preparing a teacher for National Board candidacy? Which are most within a teacher's control, and which are not? Which occur naturally and which occur by design? How can the prior experiences and readiness reported by Anne, Barbara, and Jamie help potential NBPTS candidates to prepare for the certification experience?

20.) Although their primary motivation for pursuing NBPTS certification involved the opportunity for learning through a new and unfamiliar professional challenge, all three teachers welcomed the financial support and incentives offered by their school districts and the State of Illinois. How important do you believe financial support and incentives are in motivating teachers to pursue National Board certification? Do you consider money to be more of an encouragement to potential NBPTS candidates or a reward for those who achieve the certification? Explain. What financial support and other incentives are offered through your school district and state? Do you consider these incentives to be appropriate in comparison to the time and effort required to complete the NBPTS certification process? For you personally, how important is the money on a scale of 1 to 10? Do you believe that government-funded financial support and incentives for the pursuit of National Board certification can transform the American education system? Why or why not? If not, what do you believe it will take to improve our nation's schools?

21.) In Chapter 7, the author summarizes Lustick's (2002) theory of NBPTS candidate types (pp. 148-149) before identifying Jamie as a Type D candidate. Do you agree with the author's classification? Why or why not? Do you believe that Lustick's theory is helpful in understanding variations in teacher learning during National Board candidacy? Why or why not? Of the four candidate types, which best describes your most likely experience as a potential NBPTS candidate? Explain. How can Lustick's theory help potential

NBPTS candidates to prepare for the certification experience?

22.) The three conditions that worked against Jamie during National Board candidacy were limited collaborative support, low alignment to the NBPTS standards, and a negative outlook. Which of the three conditions – support, skill, or attitude – do you believe most affects a teacher's learning through a process such as National Board certification? If Anne, Barbara, and Jamie were asked this question, which condition do you think each teacher would consider most important? Why? What can potential NBPTS candidates do to influence these conditions prior to and during National Board candidacy?

23.) Jamie experienced a great deal of difficulty representing her teaching practice through the medium of written language during National Board candidacy, and this contributed significantly to her increasing frustration and disenchantment with the process. In addition, more than one study observes that the NBPTS process is biased toward teachers who are linguistically strong (Burroughs et al., 2000; Burroughs, 2001; Lustick & Sykes, 2006; Sato, 2000: Vandevoort et al., 2004). Do you believe that the requirements for NBPTS certification should be altered to include a wider range of candidate strengths? If so, how? If these alterations were adopted by the NBPTS, what logistical problems would have to be addressed? Do you think your ideas are feasible? Why or why not?

24.) After noting Jamie's difficulty representing her teaching practice through the medium of language during National Board candidacy, the author suggests that collaborative support may have made a difference in the amount of learning that occurred for her during her certification experience as well as in earning NBPTS certification. Do you agree? Why or why not? What other factors, if any, may have altered the outcome of Jamie's certification experience? What are the most important lessons that future

National Board candidates can learn from Jamie's experience?

25.) Burroughs and colleagues (2000) classify the NBPTS certification process as a written discourse community (p. 155). Using words, a diagram, or some other medium, describe your understanding of a discourse community. Can you think of examples of written discourse communities other than National Board certification? What are some examples of discourse communities that do not rely on the written word? Are discourse communities necessary? Why or why not? In what ways do they support and hinder the learning process?

Chapter 8: The Leverage of National Board Candidacy
26.) The author defines the leverage of National Board candidacy as "an interactive dynamic between an individual and highly motivating conditions that demands teacher learning during the certification experience" (p. 162). Consider the key words and phrases in this definition: interactive, dynamic, individual, highly motivating conditions, demands, teacher learning, during. Which words stand out as most important in understanding the essence of leverage during National Board candidacy? Why do you think so? Can you think of other experiences that could be defined or described using many of the same words? If so, how are these experiences similar to or different from National Board candidacy? Based on your current understanding of the leverage of National Board candidacy, what additional words would you use to articulate its meaning?

27.) The idea of leverage expands upon other theories of teacher learning through National Board candidacy because it takes into account teachers' interaction with the NBPTS discourse. However, we learn from the experiences of Anne, Barbara, and Jamie that this interaction can be either productive, as it was with Anne and Barbara, or counterproductive, as was Jamie's experience. Is it possible for teachers to build acceptance toward the NBPTS discourse before beginning, or even during, the certification process? How might this be accomplished? If not, what alternatives are available for teachers who reject the NBPTS discourse? Do you think it is possible for teachers to reject the NBPTS discourse yet earn National Board certification? Explain.

28.) The triangles representing Anne's, Barbara's, and Jamie's leverage during National Board candidacy differ in shape and degree. The author explains that because every teacher interacts uniquely with the conditions of the certification process, the triangle representing each teacher's experience is different. Do you think there is a "typical" triangle for most National Board candidates? If so, what is it? How can understanding one's interaction with the three dynamics of leverage support a teacher during the process of National Board candidacy? Is it possible that this information could also hinder a teacher's experience? Explain.

29.) Considering the three dynamics of leverage, rigor, reward, and risk, what might your personal triangle look like during National Board candidacy? Which side would be longest? Which side would be shortest? Why do you think so? Take a few minutes to draw and label your possible triangle of leverage. Based on your knowledge about yourself as a learner, would you be more likely to try harder or to give up when confronted with the dynamic of risk? Explain. Knowing that the dynamic of risk can keep a teacher from earning NBPTS certification, what action can candidates take to minimize this dynamic during the certification experience?

Author's Note
30.) Based on the premise of social constructivism, *The Leverage of National Board Candidacy* is written so that the reader, individually or in collaboration with others, can construct her own ideas about teacher learning through the experience of NBPTS certification (see Author's Note, p. xi). Beyond simply reading the descriptions, interpretation, and analysis presented in Chapters 1 through 8, the questions

posed in the reading group guide allow the reader to reflect on the book's content through the lens of her own prior knowledge and experiences. As you read each chapter and considered or responded to the questions in the reading group guide, what prior knowledge and experiences did you most connect with? What ideas and information about teacher learning through National Board candidacy resonated with you the most? What did you disregard as irrelevant, not true, or unrealistic? Did you experience strong feelings at any point? If so, what were they and why do you think they emerged? What did you discover about yourself as a learner through reading this book and considering the accompanying questions? Has the experience changed you in any way? Explain.

References

Anderson, K., Hancock, D., & Jaus, V. (2001*). Program evaluation report for the Charlotte Collaborative Project involving the National Board for Professional Teaching Standards, Charlotte-Meeklenburg Schools, Johnson C. Smith University, and the University of North Carolina at Charlotte.* Retrieved March 20, 2003 from http://www.nbpts.org/pdf/charlotte_collaborative_rpt.pdf

Athanases, S. Z. (1994). Teachers' reports of the effects of preparing portfolios of literacy instruction. *Elementary School Journal, 94*(4), 421-439.

Beaufort, A. (1997). Operationalizing the concept of discourse community: A case study of one institutional site of composing. *Research in the Teaching of English, 31*, 486-529.

Bohen, D. B. (2001). Strengthening teaching through national certification. *Educational Leadership, 58*(8), 50-53.

Burroughs, R. (2001). The problem of National Board certification. *Journal of Teacher Education, 52*(3), 223-232.

Burroughs, R., Schwartz, T., & Hendricks-Lee, M. (2000). Communities of practice and discourse communities: Negotiating boundaries in NBPTS certification. *Teachers College Record, 102*(2), 344-374.

Center for the Future of Teaching and Learning. (2002). California teachers' perceptions of National Board certification: Individual benefits substantial, system benefits yet to be realized. Santa Cruz, CA: Author.

Chittenden, E. & Jones, J. (1997). An observational study of National Board candidates as they progress through the certification process. Paper presented at the Annual Meeting of the American Educational Research Association. (ERIC Document Reproduction Service No. ED412257)

Danielson, C. (1996). *Enhancing Professional Practice: A Framework for Teaching.* Alexandria, VA: Association for Supervision and Curriculum Development.

Darling-Hammond, L. (2001). Teacher testing and the improvement of practice. *Teaching Education, 12*(1), 11-34.

Gaddis, L. (2002). Candidate decision making through the development of the National Board for Professional Teaching Standards portfolio (Doctoral dissertation, Illinois State University, 2002). *Dissertation Abstracts International, 63*, 09A.

Glasser, W. (1997). A new look at school failure and school success. *Phi Delta Kappan, 78*(8), 596-602.

Goldhaber, D., & Anthony, E. (2004). *Can teacher quality be effectively assessed?* Retrieved June 20, 2004 from http://crpe.org/workingpapers/pdf/NBPTSquality_ report.pdf

Goldhaber, D., Perry, D., & Anthony, E. (2003). *NBPTS certification: Who applies and what factors are associated with success?* (ERIC Document Reproduction Service No. ED475841)

Hunzicker, J. L. (2003a). *Seeking, achieving, and sharing the benefits of National Board certification: An interview with a National Board certified teacher.* Unpublished manuscript.

Hunzicker, J. L. (2003b). *Conditions and characteristics that motivate and sustain teachers throughout their pursuit of National Board certification.* Unpublished manuscript.

Hunzicker, J. L. (2004). *The pursuit of National Board certification: A precipitous climb.* Unpublished manuscript.

References

Jensen, E. (1998). *Teaching with the Brain in Mind.* Alexandria, VA: Association for Supervision and Curriculum Development.

Kanter, L., Bergee, M., & Unrath, K. (2000). National Board certification in art and its potential impact on graduate programming in art education. *Arts and Learning Research Journal, 16*(1), 226-239.

Keiffer-Barone, S., Mulvaney, S., Hillman, C., & Parker, M. (1999). *Toward a professional development community: A descriptive study of the experiences of National Board candidates.* Cincinnati, OH: Paper presented at the Annual Spring Conference of the National Council of Teachers of English. (ERIC Document Reproduction Service No. ED447498)

Linquanti, R., & Peterson, J. (2001). *An enormous untapped potential: A study of the feasibility of using National Board for Professional Teaching Standards certification to improve low-performing schools.* (ERIC Document Reproduction Service No. ED462385)

Lustick, D. (2002). *National Board certification as professional development: A study that identifies a framework and findings of teachers learning to manage complexity, uncertainty, and community.* New Orleans, LA: Paper presented at the Annual Meeting of the American Educational Research Association. (ERIC Document Reproduction Service No. ED465727)

Lustick, D. & Sykes, G. (2006). National Board certification as professional development: What are teachers learning? *Education Policy Analysis Archives, 14*(5). Retrieved August 12, 2006 from http://epaa.asu.edu/apaa/v14n5/v14n5.pdf

McCarty, H. (1993). From deadwood to greenwood: Working with burned out staff. *Journal of Staff Development, 14*(1), 42-46.

Mitchell, R. D. (1998). World class teachers. *The American School Board Journal, 185* (9), 27-29.

Moseley, C., & Rains, A. (2003). National Board for Professional Teaching Standards: A reflective essay. *The Delta Kappa Gamma Bulletin, 68*(4), 44-48.

National Board for Professional Teaching Standards (2001a). *"I am a better teacher": What candidates for National Board certification say about the assessment process.* Retrieved March 20, 2003 from http://www.nbpts.org/pdf/better_teacher.pdf

National Board for Professional Teaching Standards (2001b*). Current candidate survey, September 2001(all candidates).* Retrieved March 20, 2003 from http://www.nbpts.org/pdf/cert_allcand_survey.pdf

National Board for Professional Teaching Standards (2001c). *Teachers survey data report.* Retrieved August 19, 2006 from http://www.nbpts.org/UserFiles/File/leadership_survey_data.pdf

National Board for Professional Teaching Standards (2002). *Status of National Board certified teachers in Indiana.* Retrieved August 19, 2006 from http://www.nbpts.org/UserFiles/file/indianapaper.pdf

National Board for Professional Teaching Standards (2003). *NBPTS at a glance.* Retrieved March 20, 2003 from http://www.nbpts.org/pdf/NBPTSataglance.pdf

National Board for Professional Teaching Standards (2004). *NBPTS Middle Childhood Generalist Standards: Second Edition.* Retrieved June 20, 2004 from http://www.nbpts.org/pdf/mc_gen_2ed.pdf

National Board for Professional Teaching Standards (2006). *NBCTs by Year.* Retrieved January 16, 2006 from http://www.nbpts.org/nbct/nbctdir_byyear.cfm

Pool, J., Ellet, C., Schiavone, S., & Carey-Lewis, C. (2001). How valid are the National Board of Professional Teaching Standards assessments for predicting the quality of actual classroom teaching and learning? Results of six mini case studies. *Journal of Personnel Evaluation in Education, 15*(1), 31-48.

References

Pyke, C. & Lynch, S. (2005). Mathematics and science teachers' preparation for National Board of Professional Teaching Standards certification. *School Science & Mathematics, 105*(1), 25-35.

Rotberg, I., Futrell, M., & Holmes, A. (2000). Increasing access to National Board certification. *Phi Delta Kappan, 81*(5), 379-382.

Sato, M. (2000). *The National Board for Professional Teaching Standards: Teacher learning through the assessment process.* Paper presented at the Annual Meeting of American Educational Research Association, New Orleans, LA.

Thornton, H. J. (2001). The meaning of National Board certification for middle grades teaching. *Middle School Journal, 32*(4), 46-54.

Tracz, S., Sienty, S., Todorov, K., Snyder, J., Takashima, B., Pensabene, R., Olsen, B., Pauls, L., & Sork, J. (1995). *Improvement in teaching skills: perspective from National Board for Professional Teaching Standards field test network candidates.* Paper presented at the Annual Meeting of the American Educational Research Association. (ERIC Document Reproduction Service No. ED390827)

Tracz. S., Daughtry, J., Henderson-Sparks, J., Newman, C., & Sienty, S. (2005). The impact of NBPTS participation on teacher practice: Learning from teacher perspectives. *Educational Research Quarterly, 28*(3), 35-50.

Vandevoort, L., Amrein-Beardsley, A., & Berliner, D. (2004). National Board certified teachers and their students' achievement. *Education Policy Analysis Archives, 12*(46), 1-117.

About the Author

Jana Hunzicker is an August 2006 graduate of Illinois State University (ISU) in Normal where she earned a Doctor of Education degree in Curriculum and Instruction. Intrigued by the potential of the National Board for Professional Teaching Standards (NBPTS) to improve American education, her dissertation explores the influence of the NBPTS certification process on teacher learning and student learning experiences. She holds a master's degree in Educational Administration from Bradley University in Peoria and is currently completing requirements for the Illinois superintendent's endorsement through ISU.

A native of Illinois, Dr. Hunzicker taught eighth grade language arts at Broadmoor Junior High School in Pekin District 108 for seven years before moving into school administration. Serving three years as Dean of Students at ISU's Thomas Metcalf School, she served as principal of Paul Bolin School and Neil Armstrong School in East Peoria District 86 for a total of five years, and as principal of Lincoln Grade School in Washington District 52 for one year. She has also taught part time at Illinois Central College in East Peoria.

Currently writing and consulting, Dr. Hunzicker lives in her hometown of Washington with her nephews, Tyler and Jace.

189